Ignite *your* IMPACT

The Entrepreneur's Guide to Using Facebook Ads to Build an Audience of True Believers, Make Millions of Dollars, and Spread Their Message like Wildfire

EMILY HIRSH

Dedication

For Peter (my babber) for always believing in us and our dreams.

Table of Contents

Chapter 1: Mastering Marketing for Your Business

I remember the day when one of my new clients called me and said, "It's like we're printing money! Why didn't I do this sooner?" He was referencing the Facebook ad campaign I had just turned on for him twelve hours before, and it was bringing in leads and sales faster than either of us had expected. Both of us were so excited that we could hardly sleep because refreshing the Facebook numbers was so much more exciting.

My business was less than a year old, and I was just starting to specialize in Facebook ads for my clients. I didn't have a team and I was doing everything on my own. Looking back now, I realize how much I still had to learn about Facebook ads and marketing before I would be able to masterfully serve all of our clients, but this experience was a turning point for me. I will forever be grateful that this client found me and that I had this experience. It was truly the beginning of the business I have today.

This client was the biggest client I had signed to date and he had never run ads before. His speciality was coaching other entrepreneurs to grow their business using his marketing and video strategies. He had just hit six figures in business revenue all from his organic efforts to grow his business. He reached out to me because he knew that to continue to grow his revenue and impact, he had to start using Facebook ads. When I initially got the email from him I was super nervous because I had yet to work with a client who had such a successful business. I knew that the pressure and expectations would be high and I wondered if I would be able to help him, if I was good enough for the job. He had really big goals for our time working together, and although I felt nervous, I just knew I had to take this opportunity.

He hired me and we got to work. I helped him create the entire strategy that we would run ads to and then I ran all of the Facebook ads to that strategy. We started out making just a few thousand dollars that month from our ads and then quickly realized for every $1 we were putting in, we were getting $7-$10 back out. Why not spend more? Why not spend an unlimited amount if it's bringing in that much money? I'd never seen an investment pay off the way this Facebook ad campaign was paying him.

From this career-defining experience, I learned how to scale ads and we ended up making over $100,000 in just forty-five days with $18,000 in ad spend! In addition to that, he grew his email list from 8,000 people to over 30,000 people and ended up launching a new membership site where he made an additional $30,000 in recurring monthly revenue that he didn't have before.

My mind was blown. After thirty days of working with this client, I realized I was sitting on a veritable gold mine. I knew then that I had to help others see the power of a well-thought-out marketing strategy combined with Facebook ads because this had the potential to not only change their business but change their lives. When I look back at the revenue numbers we created within that first ninety-days, I get super excited all over again about the impact that this had for my client. Before this, he had never made even close to that much money!

What I wasn't expecting was the impact that reaching this many people was going to have on my client's audience and the industry we were targeting. He had a service and product that people needed, and we would have been doing a disservice to his audience by not spending money on ads to reach new people and make sure they knew about his offer. I was lucky enough to be in the Facebook group where he grew his membership and so I was able to see the stories and testimonials of people whose lives were changed forever. On many occasions, this left me speechless and it helped me see that successful marketing is fundamentally key to building a successful business. I wish I could tell you that creating a marketing strategy that makes hundreds of thousands of dollars is always as easy as this experience, but that's not the reality. There are multiple factors that go into creating a successful marketing strategy, and although not every strategy I worked on after this made ten times the amount we spent on ads, I saw the true power that a converting marketing strategy can have on somebody's business, life, and the lives of the people they want to serve.

Without using paid ads, this client never would have been able to reach the people he did. They might have not even known that he existed! He and I have worked together for many years since, and have gone on to build his paid membership site to over 10,000 people, his email list to over 100,000 people, and his sales in the multi-millions. Those are numbers he and I couldn't even imagine when we started.

There comes a point in your business where, if you don't choose to invest in your marketing, your business will slow down and maybe even start to go backward. If you're not reaching new people, you're not growing. I've watched this happen to way too many entrepreneurs who didn't realize their full potential because they were holding themselves back. These aspiring entrepreneurs were not able to take their business to the next level because they didn't fully commit to putting themselves out there and consistently growing their audience.

I'm willing to bet that if you're reading this right now, you're not on this path to settle and just choose "good enough." You're here because of the opportunity you have to build something that you believe in, and you want to share it with the world. You're reading this book because you want the freedom to spend more time with friends and family and to have fun, all on your own terms. You're here because you deeply desire the abundance that smashing your sales goals and growing your business to seven figures will bring you. You're here because you're ready to claim your place as a 21st century thought leader in your industry. You're here because what makes you happier than anything are the moments where you get to live your purpose and make a powerful impact in the world.

Strategic marketing is not just a way to make more money (even though when done right, you'll make a lot of it). It's also the fastest path to greater impact and changing lives. Once I realized that a converting marketing strategy had the potential to reach thousands or even millions of people within a matter of days, I dedicated my own business and time to mastering successful marketing strategies for my clients. I've now been fortunate to be behind the scenes of millions of dollars in ad spend and revenue generated from Facebook ads. I've also been fortunate enough to teach many entrepreneurs how to create a marketing strategy who had never run Facebook ads before.

I've put in over 10,000 hours into mastering digital marketing and creating systems and processes that bring companies enormous success. I don't just do this because I love marketing, although I do. I do this because I love watching the impact that successful marketing has on an entrepreneur and on their audience.

After obsessing over what strategies and processes create successful marketing, I've cracked the code to mastering both profit and impact using paid marketing strategies. In this book I will show you exactly how to crack that code for your own business. I can't wait to take this journey with you!

Chapter 2: From $18/Hour to $3M in Four Years!

Not long ago, I was twenty years old and living with my husband in our 600 square-foot studio. I had to take client calls in this little hallway outside of the studio because it was too loud inside of my house to take them. I didn't know what I was doing, nor did I realize the extent of the business potential that was right in front of my eyes.

I was a young mom, didn't have a college degree or a stable job at the time, and I felt like I was doing everything wrong. I eventually dropped out of college and never looked back because I realized my business was growing faster than I could keep up with. Something had to give.

I was supposed to be this big failure because of these things, according to society and all of the judgment I had around me. Yet, in four years, I have taken my company, which started just with me as a virtual assistant making $18 an hour, to a $3M marketing agency and a team of thirty employees and over sixty clients.

You might be reading this wondering how I managed to pull this off. In fact, the most common question I get asked in interviews and when speaking about my business is, "how have you built this company, what's your secret?"

The truth is, there is no secret to my success. From day one, finding out I was 19 and pregnant, I made a decision. I made a decision that no matter what, I was going to make this work and I was not just going to survive but I was going to thrive. I strongly believed that I got to choose the outcome of my future and I didn't have to let what everyone else was telling me become my reality. Most of the beginning of my journey, I didn't know what I was doing and I didn't have a huge plan. I took it one day at a time and I continued to work hard, stay determined and followed what was working and gaining momentum.

I started as a virtual assistant doing basic admin tasks. I would teach myself all of the different online softwares and platforms I needed to help my clients. Each client I worked with gave me new experiences that I leveraged and used to grow and find the next client. After awhile I knew dozens of online softwares and platforms and I was completely booked with clients wanting me to help them. It was then that I started doing Facebook ads and marketing for these clients. As soon as I started working on these marketing and Facebook ad campaigns for my clients and seeing amazing results, I knew I had found my future.

When I started my company, it was just me running ads for our clients. That worked for a while, but eventually, I knew I wanted to grow my business much bigger and would need to hire and train a team to do that. Hiring and training was something I had never done before and I had no idea where to start. I made a lot of mistakes, hired people out of desperation for help but didn't set them up for success because I wasn't clear on exactly what kind of help I needed. After a few stressful experiences I started finding the right people to support me and realized I needed to come up with a way to teach my team what I was doing for our clients. The problem was that what I was doing felt intuitive to me. I didn't know how to put it into words, let alone create training videos to teach somebody else.

I had personally been behind the scenes of many successful marketing campaigns and all of that experience gave me a very unique view on marketing. I had strategies and methods that I'd proven worked for many different clients. However, at the time, I didn't know how to communicate what I was doing well enough to teach other people. I thought to myself many times, "Nobody else can do what I do with our clients."

I was completely wrong with this thought. It took a mentor of mine to point out that what I was doing was not so unique and special that it couldn't be replicated with the right process and training. I was engaged in a consulting day with a mentor working specifically on improving and streamlining my business and I said to him, "I just don't think anybody can do what I do." These words became my famous statement because in the moment I believed what I was saying was true but over time I was proven fundamentally wrong. This mentor explained to me that no CEO is so special that they can't streamline and synthesize what they are doing and communicate it to their team members. It took quite a bit of convincing on his part but eventually I came to understand that if I was going to expand my company, I'd have to at least attempt to train a team to do what I was doing for clients.

This is how *The Hirsh Process* was born. After that consulting meeting I locked myself in a room until I had fully documented the way I understand both Facebook ads as well as marketing strategies. I mapped out the process I was using to help my clients achieve success over and over again. I didn't stop refining the process until it was so basic and so clear that I could explain it to anyone regardless of their previous experience. It took me a couple of months to fully master this but soon I had created a process that I could not only train new team members with but also share with others so they too could better understand marketing. I used this process to train new ads managers to manage our client accounts so I could continue to grow my business. Today, it's expanded into a 90 day training program all our new team members go through as well as material that I share through speaking and writing with my audience.

All of the marketing decisions I would make to bring success to my clients felt natural to me, but the reality is that I wasn't born with some special secret or intuition that nobody else has. It wasn't until I saw people around me in various communities trying but not seeing the success that I realized maybe I was doing something different that I could help others with.

Not only was I creating a successful company myself, but I was also surrounded by my clients having tons of success. I questioned myself more about what contributes to the success and what holds people back from success. Now, when I'm asked this question, I have a lot of answers and advice that I can give, because I've learned how to analyze my journey and other entrepreneurs paths as well, to see where they were hitting their mark and where they made mistakes. I will share a lot of these with you throughout this book, so you can learn from my experience.

Out of all of the different factors that I believe contributed to my success, there are three core values I've found that are the most important. I grew my business with them and was able to build outstanding client relationships.

The Three Core Values:

1. Deliver something valuable and meaningful
2. Connect with your audience/ customer
3. Always live up to your word

To make this even simpler, we can boil this down to two very important words: *connection* and *value.*

Creating connection and providing value to customers should be the number one priority for most businesses. It doesn't matter if you offer digital products, physical products, or services, if you prioritize these two things, you will grow your business. I've watched dozens of entrepreneurs who prioritize these succeed and I've watched dozens of entrepreneurs who don't prioritize them have a really hard time achieving their goals.

I'm extremely proud of the $21M in Facebook ad spend our company has managed in the last few years, which has generated over $100M in client revenue. What all of that ad spend equals are experience and perspective. I've spent the last few years building my team and becoming an observer of everything happening in my business and everything happening with our clients. This opportunity has given me a perspective that I think very few people have about the industry. I've been able to see behind the scenes of over one hundred entrepreneurs' businesses and take all of that experience and intel and learn from it. In the last year, I've seen a huge shift in the online marketing industry. I've watched successful entrepreneurs who were making money and "living the dream" go backward, and some, sadly, have even lost everything.

Here is what I've discovered: Companies who have maintained their connection with their audience, who care about providing value to their audience and delivering an end product that works will grow and maintain authority in their industry. The secret to marketing success is not marketing hacks that will convince people to buy your offer. It's not getting millions of video views or "funnel hacking" the experts to then replicate what they do in your own business. The secret to marketing success is to never lose sight of the value you provide your audience and the connection you build with them every day. If you can do that, marketing and building your business will feel simple, straightforward and will result in profitability, impact, and satisfied customers.

I'm going to show you all of the different strategies to a successful marketing campaign that I've gathered and learned from supporting our clients at Hirsh Marketing, as well as building my business to $3M. As I do that, I want you to remember, that at the core of every strategy, building and maintaining your connection with your audience is the most important.

Chapter 3: The Hirsh Process at a High Level

The *he Hirsh Process* started with the only purpose being to train my team as I grew to over ten ad managers and sixty clients on our roster. We documented the process and then we made training materials with it that taught new team members how we did it, so they could also serve our clients. I got a lot of feedback from team members going through the training. They told me it was some of the best training they had ever been through. They were not starting from scratch. The people I trained were marketers with quite a bit of previous experience, I realized then that my process could help a lot of people if I started teaching my audience publicly. Since then I have taught thousands of people *The Hirsh Process* through podcasts, videos, blog posts, speaking on stage, and even in our digital training program. *The Hirsh Process* is not just how you set up your Facebook ads, but it's a way to look at every piece of your marketing from beginning to end. It's a very clear and direct way to understand each phase of your marketing, regardless of your marketing experience.

The Hirsh Process covers every step you need to create and optimize a successful marketing campaign that is customized for your own business. It doesn't matter if you're already making a million dollars or you're just starting, everything in this process is relevant to a successful marketing campaign and will be relevant for your own business. Every business that sells something has a customer journey, also known as a sales funnel. That customer journey might have several steps to it or it might be as simple as going to your website and buying your product. Our process and the rest of this book is about creating a strategic journey that will attract customers and sales to your business consistently.

I'm so excited to teach you the revolutionary *Hirsh Process* and my goal is for it to help you get super clear about what you need to focus on in your own business to create a marketing strategy that makes both an impact and money. I will be diving into each of these 5 Steps in much more detail but for now let me give you a high level view of this process.

Step 1: Strategize

The first step of *The Hirsh Process* is everything you need to do before you start running ads. In this step, we're going to walk through three different questions you will need to answer to set a solid foundation for the rest of your marketing.

When I teach this process, many people expect me to dive straight into the actual Facebook ads piece. I don't because the foundation you create before running your ads will determine the success of your ads. Creating strategy around your foundation and starting your marketing with a solid understanding of who you're trying to market to, how you're going to communicate to them and how you're going to attract them to what you sell is a core component of a successful marketing strategy.

I've seen way too many people skip this pre-work and have to come back to it after wasting thousands of dollars and weeks of their time. This pre-work is not easy and takes time and effort, but it's crucial to your marketing success and should not be skipped.

Step 2: Brand Awareness and Visibility

Building an online brand and loyal following is a core piece to a successful marketing strategy and is often overlooked. Many people focus on the number of followers you have on your Instagram account or the number of viewers you get on your videos, but those numbers are just vanity metrics and actually don't matter very much.

What matters is that you're building a loyal following of people who want to buy what you sell. The way you build a loyal following is by consistently prioritizing valuable content you can deliver to your audience. This can be in the form of podcasts, videos, blogs or social media posts. In this step, I am going to teach you how to commit to a brand awareness strategy that is right for your business and will help you build a loyal audience of not only followers, but also paying customers.

Step 3: Lead Generation

Lead generation is where some businesses will spend up to eighty percent of their ad budget and is a crucial piece to marketing success. This step's goal is to capture people's information, such as their name and email address, to then nurture them further down your customer journey and ultimately sell them what you offer. If you're an ecommerce business, selling a physical product, you will probably spend twenty percent of your ad budget on this step. If you sell a service or a digital product such as an online course or coaching program, you will probably spend eighty percent of your ad budget here.

There are a few huge mistakes people make in this step, including creating a lead generation strategy that isn't strategic for their audience or their business. I will show you how to create a customized lead generation strategy for your audience, based on highly converting strategies that both myself and clients have used. I will also help you nail down your targeting so you can get inexpensive leads that are quality customers.

Step 4: Make Money

Once you make it to this step, you're successfully gathering email leads and trying to turn them into a paying customer. People often lack in their follow-up in this step and end up losing a lot of money.

You've worked so hard to get your leads this far into your funnel and now there are a few small but effective strategies you can implement to get the most out of your hard work and investment this far.

I will share with you some of our most effective strategies for making sure leads turn into paying customers in both your email and retargeting ad strategies. In this step we will look at different ads you can use that don't cost a lot but can greatly increase your marketing return. We have several follow up strategies we use for our clients that in some cases have doubled and tripled the money they are making back on their marketing.

Step 5: Scale and Optimize

After you've started running ads and you're taking email leads through a customer journey you strategically created, you're also getting data. That data is going to tell you if your strategy is working or not. If you're strategic with how you look at the data, it will also tell you exactly what you need to focus on to get your strategy to convert.

In this step, I am going to not only tell you exactly what you need to track, but also what to do if one of the numbers or steps in your strategy is not converting. Once you optimize your strategy and ads so they're profitable, then it will be time to scale.

Your ultimate goal with your marketing is to create an ATM, that will spit out more money than you put in day in and day out. You can't confidently do that without knowing your numbers, and this step of *The Hirsh Process* will help you understand what numbers to look at, and then what decisions to make with those numbers once you have them.

Constantly Revisiting These Steps

It doesn't matter if you're a beginner or an advanced marketer, these steps will be relevant to you. Oftentimes, you'll go through these steps and find something you need to implement or fix right away, and then you'll go through them again on a later date and find something new. The data will always point you in the right direction from beginning to end.

The Hirsh Process will help you look at your marketing strategy, and will highlight exactly what you need to focus on right now for the best results. If you follow every one of these steps and constantly come back to them to fine-tune your strategy, you will successfully create a profitable marketing strategy, without the overwhelm and frustration many people experience.

Chapter 4: What To Do Before You Start Running Ads

I've been behind the scenes of hundreds of ad campaigns with ad budgets ranging from $500 to over $1M. No matter what level you're at, there is a foundation that needs to be set before you ever spend a penny on your ads. This foundation is arguably more important than the actual ad campaigns, and if you skip these core steps, you will struggle to see success in your marketing and probably waste a lot of money in the process.

There are three main components to set your marketing strategy foundation, and we are going to go over each one in detail:

- Mastering your messaging, who you're speaking to, and the problem you solve
- Mastering your strategy so it's tailored to your audience
- Mastering your numbers and setting your goals

Each one of these is crucial to a successful marketing strategy. I have seen successful, seven-figure business owners missing these components and losing money because of it, and I don't want that to happen to you. So, let's set your foundation so everything you build on top of it will be successful.

Mastering Your Messaging, Who You're Speaking To, and The Problem You Solve

I always tell people that you can have the best strategy in the entire world, but if your messaging is off, nothing will work. Messaging is everything. If you can't connect to the people you're trying to attract into your business, you will constantly struggle to get people to see you and hear your message. Don't skip over messaging and jump into creating your strategy, because the strategy can't exist without your messaging being fine-tuned.

The most important piece to getting clear on your messaging is first getting clear on *exactly* who you're speaking to. Narrow it down to one person, and create a profile description of this person so that, in the future, when you're writing ad copy or creating a podcast, you remember who you're talking to. This person should originate from who you're going to sell your product or service to.

Write the most detailed description you can of this person. What do they google when they have a question? What keeps them up at night? What are they afraid of? What are they most proud of? Everything you can think of to create a very clear and detailed picture of this person. It can be somebody real or somebody you make up, but regardless, make them a relatable and specific person in your head.

A lot of times when I suggest this, it brings up fears for people that they will lose potential customers because they are not speaking to them in addition to their ideal customer persona. You won't. Naturally, your content is going to attract more than just the ideal persona you create, but it's incredibly powerful to be clear on a single persona and speak directly to them. This allows you to be direct, it allows you to be polarizing, and most importantly, it allows you to stand out from everyone else.

If you're speaking to everybody, you're speaking to nobody. Say that a few times and then never forget it. I know it's hard to feel like you're saying "no" to certain people or groups, but this has been proven hundreds of times over. It's so much more effective and powerful to be specific and direct with who you're speaking to in all of your content and marketing. This is the only way you will be able to connect and get through to your audience in a way that will grow your business and impact.

Once you know who you're speaking to, you have to clearly define the problem your business solves for that person. If somebody in conversation was to ask you right now, "What problem do you solve for people?", would you have a clear answer? It's okay if you don't. It's often hard for people to articulate this, but I want you to work on this. Believe me, specificity changes everything!

The key to being able to define and communicate the problem you solve for your ideal customer is that you define it in a way they would say it themselves. Let's use my business as an example: I help driven entrepreneurs create paid marketing strategies that make money and create impact. That's a clear statement because my ideal customer would easily be caught saying something in casual conversation like, *"I need help strategizing a paid marketing strategy that makes me money."*

I could easily complicate this statement with

language I understand, but my ideal customer would *not* be caught saying: "I help entrepreneurs create sales funnels and Facebook ad campaigns that convert and bring positive ROI." The statements mean the same thing, but the second example is not how my ideal customer would speak. Therefore, they would not connect with this language in my marketing. Make sure to create a statement about the problem you solve and write it in the way that your ideal customer would speak.

Once you're clear on the ideal customer you're speaking to and the problem you solve, you will need to constantly remind yourself of these two things when creating any content, both free and paid. It's crucial that when you create free content such as blog posts, podcasts, and videos, you're still speaking to this person and communicating the problem you solve, even if it's indirectly. This allows you to attract your potential buyer, no matter what form you're doing it in.

We will talk more about creating free content that builds an audience of buyers in the next chapter. For now, keep in mind that if somebody listens to a podcast episode of yours or watches your video on Instagram and doesn't understand the problem you solve, then it isn't clear enough. This doesn't mean you're pitching your services directly, it means that what you're teaching relates to the problem you solve. You want to be so clear that a brand new customer who doesn't know your brand would be able to understand exactly what you offer in your business and how you could potentially help them.

For example, if I made a bunch of podcast episodes about how to live a healthy life as a mom and a CEO and somebody new came along and listened to those with no prior knowledge to my brand, they might think I am a coach helping moms become healthier. This would be very confusing to those new listeners to then have me pitch marketing services. Make sure your content is cohesive and, even if it's valuable free content, it's still attracting your potential buyers.

Mastering Your Strategy So It's Tailored to Your Audience

Once you know who you are trying to attract, you'll need to create a strategy that will attract your ideal customer most effectively. This will become your *customer journey* or your *sales funnel,* and it's crucial that what we create is custom to your business and your audience.

I've helped strategize hundreds of different marketing strategies and a huge mistake I watch happen all the time is somebody goes to an event, watches a successful influencer speak about their strategy that made them a million dollars, and then they come back and replicate that strategy exactly in their business. This also happens when people buy courses and replicate exactly what is being taught in that course for their business, without giving themselves any room to consider that their business is different and might require a few changes to the strategy being taught.

This is never the fault of the individual who takes a strategy and replicates it. In my opinion, it's the responsibility of the course creator or the influencer to make sure people understand that this strategy worked for them because it was created and perfected for their business and audience, not because it's a secret strategy that, if everyone copies it, they will see guaranteed success. It's okay to take a framework and implement it in your own marketing, but you must be able to consider your audience and business and make changes where they are needed, based on those factors.

There are two key components to consider when creating your strategy:

1. Your audience and how they will most effectively be taken from a cold lead, who doesn't know you, to a paying customer
2. Your product and the price point of your product

Let's talk about both of these a bit deeper so that by the end of this you're clear on a strategy that is most effective for your business.

Your Audience

Considering your audience when creating your strategy is crucial. If you're targeting business owners and entrepreneurs with your marketing, they will most likely make decisions faster and need less overall nurturing before becoming a customer. On the other hand, business owners are also bombarded with content, so if you're driving them to a webinar or a PDF download, you will probably pay more for those leads, but make up for it with a higher sales conversion once they are consuming your content. If you're targeting consumers, it's most likely going to be the opposite. They will sign up for your free webinar or video at a very cheap cost, but take a lot more nurturing to become a customer because they don't typically make investment decisions quickly.

I once had a client come to me after going to a mastermind event. She declared that she was going to create a paid challenge for $27 to target her audience of moms who want to lose weight because everyone in her mastermind was doing it and it was working for them. As soon as I heard this, I knew it wouldn't work, so I coached her through it. I knew that the group of people she got advice from was filled with people targeting other business owners, and she was targeting moms who want to lose weight. Moms who want to lose weight are probably not going to pay $27 just to participate in a challenge when they don't even know the brand and they are also bombarded with free challenge offers from other companies all the time.

We decided to stick with her original plan of a free challenge, which then promoted her membership site to all challenge participants. It converted wonderfully, and led to over six-figures in sales. Had she followed "everyone else" with the cookie-cutter strategy they were teaching, she would have wasted a lot of time and money trying to make it work.

We will get into more specific detail about all the customer journey options you can choose for your audience in a later chapter, but for now, I want you to be thinking of your funnel or your customer journey as just that, a journey.

How are you going to take somebody who has never heard of your brand before and turn them into a paying customer? What experience do they need to have to build trust with you and your company, and ultimately decide giving you their money is the best possible decision they can make? If you know your audience is super busy, consider that. If you know your audience will need a lot of nurturing, consider that too. Start thinking about it so that when I share with you some of the top converting strategies you will know how to take those and customize it for your ideal buyer.

Your Product

The second key thing we have to consider when creating a strategy is the price of your product. The higher the price, the more nurturing you will need in your strategy because the more trust it's going to take to turn a potential buyer into a paying customer. If you're selling a $400 product, you don't need as many touchpoints with your brand as you would if you were selling a $1,997 product. Nurturing people in your marketing strategy is essentially building trust with them. You can build trust through strategic videos, emails, webinars, or experiences you take somebody through, such as a challenge or video series.

Think about how much nurturing you need to include in your strategy, based on the price of your product. This way, when I share top converting strategies, you will be able to easily choose one and create a strategy with enough touchpoints that it effectively turns people from a cold lead to a paying customer.

Mastering Your Numbers and Setting Your Goals

I was recently speaking in front of a room of seven, eight, and even nine-figure business owners, and I asked this question to the audience: "How many of you right now could either tell me the answer or easily find the answer to the following questions: How many email leads are you trying to bring in every month with your marketing? How many sales are you expecting to get from those leads? How much are you spending to accomplish all of this?" Three out of one hundred people raised their hands. *Three percent* of the room! These people are successful entrepreneurs, making millions of dollars, and many of them don't have a specific understanding of the numbers in the way that they could maximize their success.

Defining Success

If you take away one thing from this book, I want it to be what I am about to teach you. If you can learn how to think of marketing as numbers and force yourself to fully understand your numbers, even if you hate it and it goes against everything you want to do, you will be wildly successful. To run successful ads and have a marketing strategy that makes money, you first have to define what success means to you and your business. If we don't define success, then we will never know if we are achieving it or not.

I never again want you to have thoughts about your marketing such as, "I have no idea if this is working or not." If you define success before you spend a penny on ads, then you will always know if it's working or not. In addition to knowing if it's working, you will also know what isn't working, so you can immediately start to fix it. My team will never turn on a client's ads without going through all of these steps and having solid numbers defined and communicated. I want the same for you.

Many experts will tell you to start with deciding your ad budget as one of the first questions you answer. You may have talked to somebody before about running ads and one of the first questions they ask is, "How much do you want to spend this month?" The problem is, you can't answer this question correctly without first working backward and answering what your goals are. Your budget is based on what you're trying to get out of that budget, and should only be determined by your sales goal, not a made-up number in your head that you guessed.

Here are the steps to defining success in your marketing strategy (reference page 105 in the back of the book for more in depth exercises on setting your budget):

1. Decide how much money you want to make selling your product or service in one month (choose only one offer here, if you have multiple offers then you have to go through these steps for each one).

2. Take how much money you want to make and divide it by the cost of your product or service. This number gives you the amount of units or customers you will need to sell in that month.

3. Now, if three percent of all the email leads you bring in purchase your offer, how many leads do you need to bring onto your list in one month?

4. Let's say you will pay an average cost of $4 per email

lead you add to your list, multiply that by the number above and that is your monthly ad spend. I've created a calculator for you to play with your own numbers and walk through these steps until you're clear, you can download that calculator here: www.fbadcalculator.com

In the steps above I used "average" numbers, but you can adjust the numbers in steps 3 and 4 based on your industry and offer. If your product is high priced, you might make it one percent of all your leads who are expected to buy. Or, if you're targeting an audience that converts at a cheaper cost per lead, such as moms who want to lose weight, you might consider changing your average cost per lead to somewhere around $2.

An average cost per email lead is typically $1-$10 depending on what the lead is being driven to and who you are targeting. If you're sending people to an opt-in where there is not much of a commitment such as an ebook or PDF download, it will probably be around $1-$4. If you're sending people to a webinar or a video series where they have a bigger time commitment, it will probably cost more like $4-$10 for each email lead. If you're targeting business owners, you will usually pay more cost per lead, and if you're targeting consumers, you will typically pay less. For example, a business coach targeting other entrepreneurs will typically pay a higher cost per lead than somebody targeting moms who want to lose weight.

It's important to note here that the goal is not to get the cheapest cost per lead but instead to get a quality lead. Choosing a low commitment lead generation strategy just to get the cheapest cost per lead will sometimes backfire when it comes time to sell your offer and the sales conversion is lower. Your goal is to choose a customer journey and lead generation strategy that makes sense for your offer and audience.

Some industry averages worth considering for your sales conversion from these email leads are that one to five percent of the leads you bring in typically purchase what you're offering. The higher the price of your offer, the lower the percentage usually is. The audience you're targeting also impacts this conversion. If you're targeting business owners, this percentage is often a bit higher, and if you're targeting consumers, this percentage is usually lower.

Below is a table of industry averages for both cost per leads and sales conversions for different industries and strategies:

	B2C MARKET	B2B MARKET
COST PER LEAD		
Lead Magnet	$1.00 - $3.00	$2.50 - $5.00
Quiz	$0.50 - $3.00	$2.50 - $4.00
Challenge	$1.00 - $3.00	$2.50 - $5.00
Webinar	$3.00 - $5.00	$5.00 - $10.00
Video Series	$3.00 - $5.00	$5.00 - $7.00
Application	$100-$150	$100-$250
SALES CONVERSION (the higher the price of your product, the lower the sale conversion will most likely be)		
Webinar	0.5% - 1% of all leads	1% - 3% of all leads
Video Series	0.5% - 1% of all leads	1% - 3% of all leads
Challenge	0.5% - 1% of all leads	1% - 3% of all leads
Call Applications	3% - 5% of all leads will apply	5-10% of all leads will apply

If you've never run ads before, you won't have any data to go off of and will need to use averages to answer these questions. Once you start running ads, you will be able to plug these numbers in with some more solid data, specific to your business, which is the ultimate goal.

At the end of this exercise, you should have the following numbers defined for your first month of ads:

- How much money you will make
- How many sales you will sell in units
- How many leads you need to bring onto your list
- How much you will spend to accomplish all of this

If you go through these steps and initially feel like you're not comfortable spending the budget you have to to reach your goals, that's okay; it happens all the time and it's part of why we do this exercise so we can be honest with ourselves from the beginning. If this happens, all you need to do is go back through the steps and adjust until what you are comfortable spending reflects realistic goals of what you will achieve with that budget. This exercise will kill the false hope of making six-figures with a $2,000 ad spend because the numbers will never add up.

If you're still overwhelmed with this exercise and setting up your marketing goals, my team and I offer video trainings and live coaching around this in our program Ignite which you can get access to here: www.ignitecourse.com

Let's run through a real-life scenario here, so you can see this play out:

Our client has a $1,000 product that targets other entrepreneurs and shows them how to launch a digital course. We go through this exercise with her.

We decide that in the first thirty days of running

ads, she wants to make $5,000.

Based on that number, she needs to sell five courses

If two percent of all the leads on her email list buy, she needs to add 250 leads to her list.

If her average cost per lead is $5 she needs to spend $1,250 to get 250 leads and make her $5,000

Now, we have metrics to measure her success and we have goals to aim for when starting her ads. If we start running ads, and her email leads are costing $7 then we know we are off and need to optimize the ads themselves to get the cost down. If we are getting leads at a great cost per lead, but nobody is buying, we need to look at the strategy and the way her offer is being pitched so we can optimize and improve that. After we run ads for the first thirty days, we will have some more real data, and we can choose to change the numbers and our projections for the next thirty days, based on that data.

If all of these numbers overwhelm you, my team has made a calculator where you can plug your numbers in and play around with the different averages at each step, to ultimately get your ad budget and goals calculated for you. You can download that calculator here: www.fbad-calculator.com

Your marketing strategy will only be as good as the foundation you build first. Having a crystal clear picture of your ideal customer, the problem you solve for them and defining goals and metrics to your strategy will provide you with a solid foundation to build on top of.

Chapter 5: Use Your Free Content to Attract Buyers

One of the biggest powers of social media is the ability to build a loyal following and connect with potential buyers through the content you share on platforms such as Facebook, Instagram, your website, or other social media channels. This content can be in the form of videos, blogs, podcasts, or social media posts and stories where the main purpose is for you to share something of value that will attract people to your business and begin building trust with your brand.

At its core, marketing is about connection and building trust. If you can strategically and effectively connect with your audience, you will be successful in selling to them and therefore grow your business. If you don't put any effort or attention into creating a connection with your audience, you will struggle to grow your business and build trust. It doesn't matter what you sell, people will buy if they feel a connection with your brand and what you're offering.

Creating Valuable Content to Build Your Brand

The most effective way to build trust and a loyal following is by delivering free, valuable content that can be easily accessed by a large number of people. I suggest that you choose one medium and one platform which will help you connect with people and which plays to your strengths. For example, if you hate video but you're great at writing, use blogs. If you're great with video (or even just okay at it, because I know almost nobody thinks they are amazing at filming video) and people connect with you, use video and choose one main way you will use it, such as Facebook live. Once you decide on your media and platform you need to make sure you show-up consistently.

In my own company, I connect with people primarily through my podcast. I release two episodes every week, across my top social media platforms. My podcast is filled with free, valuable content that gives people actionable advice they can use to improve their business. In every episode, I speak directly to my ideal customer, and, over time, this helps me build trust with my audience so that ultimately, buying our services is an easy decision for them.

After working with hundreds of different brands and watching people show up differently online, I can tell you, hands down, creating consistent, valuable content will grow your business faster than anything else. Creating content is one thing we can't do for our clients because it typically requires the face of the brand to record the podcast episodes, or create the videos, and some prioritize this better than others. When I compare the clients who do prioritize this to the ones who don't, I see a massive difference in results, every single time. The clients who do prioritize this typically see cheaper email leads, grow their business faster, get more sales, and have more successful product launches.

We recently started working with a huge influencer,

who, up until hiring us, had only relied on organic traffic to grow their business. They had created, by far, the most successful business and brand I had ever seen that hadn't spent any money on ads yet. When I told them how incredible their results were, they said, "Want to know the key? It's our daily live video we do."

That simple. Show up consistently. Deliver value. Connect with your audience and you will not only grow a large number of followers, but you will grow a loyal following, and that is hard to put a price on. Growing a loyal audience of followers that deeply value both you and your content, and also truly believe in everything you create, makes selling easy. There is nothing that can take that away from your brand once you build it, and it only comes from constantly connecting and building your audience for, not days or months, but for years.

If you have ever thought that successful marketing is some version of creating one funnel or strategy, getting it out there, and then allowing sales to come in only by creating that one strategy, I want you to get that idea out of your head. It's the most unsustainable and unrealistic way to look at marketing and building a business.

Building a real business that will be around for not just a year but for decades is about the long game. It's about creating followers and trust that builds on top of each other and eventually becomes a snowball that gains traction and speed. A sustainable business is built with an audience of loyal followers that, no matter what, will be there and continue to grow.

It's critical that what you create is not just to create something, but that it also attracts buyers. Remember, if somebody consumes just one piece of your content, they should still know what problem your business solves, even though you won't be directly selling anything.

Don't make the mistake of creating content and putting in all that time to then find out you successfully attracted people, but they aren't potential buyers. Reference back to the ideal persona that you created in the previous chapter and make sure anything you create to grow your brand and connect with your audience is also going to attract potential customers. Connect with that person as you plan out what content you're going to create.

I also want you to consider that ideal customer when thinking about the form of content you're going to create. If your audience is extremely busy, don't choose sixty-minute long podcast episodes or videos they will never have time to listen to or watch. If your audience most likely hates to read, don't choose lengthy blog posts to send them to. Create content that is easy for them to consume so they do consume it.

Committing to Creating Your Content

The first step to mastering your brand awareness and visibility is choosing how you're going to connect with people. Is it video, writing, or voice?

If you automatically choose writing to be your form of content while reading this, I want you to think twice and make sure you're not choosing the easier, more comfortable route, but you're choosing the most effective. Nobody is one hundred percent comfortable on video, but using a form of video or voice is typically more effective than writing because it's a different level of connection for the audience to hear and see you.

Eventually, you will probably create content in several different forms as you grow your brand, but for now, I want you to choose one and I want you to choose one that might make you a little uncomfortable, but you're going to push your comfort zone and do it anyway. Don't try to choose more than one because it's really hard to master everything at once and it won't set you up for success.

The second step is choosing the realistic frequency at which you will create this content. Is it twice a week? Once a week? Ideally, it's at least once a week, because that is the minimum frequency you need to always stay top of mind for your audience. However, notice how I said realistic frequency. Don't choose every day or five times a week if you know that is just setting you up for failure, based on how much time you have to commit. Quality content is better than quantity, so set yourself up for success.

Once you know these two things, the final step is writing a statement that commits to both the form of content you will create and the frequency at which you create it.

Here are some examples of how this could look:

1. "I will release two podcast episodes a week."

2. "I will do a Facebook live video every Tuesday and Thursday"

3. "I will release a blog post one time a week"

4. "I will post a content video twice a week"

Commit to your statement and then calendar-in time where you will accomplish it. Hold yourself accountable to this content and showing up for your audience in this way. It's not easy, but it's crucial to your marketing success.

Getting Eyes on Your Valuable Content

Once you're creating content and consistently posting it on your platforms, we have to combine ad spend with your content to get new eyes on it. Unfortunately, the way the algorithms are set up today, it's nearly impossible to count on organic reach to grow your following, because it won't reach many new people if any. You can rapidly grow a loyal audience by combining a small amount of ad spend with the content you're already working hard to create, and I'm going to show you how.

Let's say you create a Facebook live on your business page and you get fifty viewers because, let's be real, you just started this business page and half of your likes are family members supporting you. Don't give up on the whole process and think creating content is not going to work for you because you can't get eyes on it. It will.

Once you create your content, you're going to turn it into a paid Facebook ad and target people who have never heard of you before but are your ideal audience of potential buyers. The best way to strategize this targeting is to use pages that your ideal customer may follow, and target followers of those pages.

For example, if you're trying to target entrepreneurs, you could target people who like *Entrepreneur Magazine* or Gary Vaynerchuck. If you're trying to target people who follow the Paleo diet, you could target people who follow big influencers in that community, such as The Paleo Mom. Think about your ideal customer and brainstorm some pages they follow to use as your targeting. Everyone you think of will probably not be an option to target on Facebook, but this will be a great start at reaching new people.

You don't need a lot in your ad budget to make this effective. We typically recommend five to ten percent of your monthly ad budget goes to your brand awareness and visibility ads. This means, if you're spending $2,500 per month on your marketing, you would spend an additional $75-$250 per month promoting your content to new audiences.

Some examples of how this may look are if you chose video as your form of content, you would put the video on your Facebook business page and promote the video directly. If you chose blog posts or podcasts, you would create an ad, driving people to your website where that blog post is or that podcast episode is posted. If you're sending somebody off of Facebook or Instagram, you must make sure you're sending them to your website, where you have placed a Facebook pixel and are capturing the data of people clicking your ad. You can't place a Facebook pixel on a site that you don't own, like iTunes, so send your traffic to a site you own where you can place the pixel.

Pixels can be overwhelming, but what you need

to remember here is that, if your content is a video or post, put it directly on your Facebook business page and promote that directly. If it's a blog or podcast and you're sending them off Facebook, send them to a page you own and have already pixeled before running the ad.

If you need help placing a pixel on your website we created a free basic training for you that can be downloaded here: www.howtoplaceapixel.com

Once you start turning your content into paid ads, you are not only building followers and an audience that is connecting with you, but you're also creating audiences you can use strategically in the future. In the next chapter, we are going to talk about getting actual email leads and contact information into your funnel. Once you get to that step, you're going to be able to use the audiences you built here to target your next steps in your customer journey.

If you've been promoting videos on your Facebook page in the past, you now have an audience of people who have watched various lengths of those videos. If you have been sending people to your website, you now have an audience of people who have clicked those ads and landed on your website. This particular audience is considered warm traffic. If you target them to the next steps of your customer journey, they will most likely convert at a lower cost, and, even more importantly, they will be a higher quality lead because they have already begun building trust with your brand by consuming your content.

Many companies make the mistake of thinking that building followers means paying for likes or followers on their social media, and that's the first ads they choose to spend money on. Don't worry if you've done this, many people have. However, this is not effective or recommended. If somebody saw an ad to like your page, they may have liked it, but they have no idea who you are, and they don't have any connection to your brand. Therefore, they will most likely not turn into a loyal follower, let alone a paying customer. When you create "like ads" for followers, you're also telling Facebook to get you likes for the lowest cost, which typically means you're getting people who like thousands of pages and are not quality followers. It's so much more effective to take your budget and put it into promoting your content, where your audience will connect with you and you can begin to build that relationship.

Strategically, growing your brand and your audience with free content, and then pairing that free content with a small amount of ad spend, is the most effective way to build an audience of loyal followers that can then easily be taken to the next steps of your customer journey. Combining ad spend with your content is also a much faster way at building your following and brand awareness, rather than posting on social media and hoping people will see it, which will for sure result in slow progress and frustration.

Once you have a clear commitment on the type of content you're going to create, the frequency you will release it, and the budget you will spend promoting it, you're ready to move on to mastering your lead generation and getting actual email leads and people through your funnel!

If at anytime you're feeling overwhelmed and you'd

like more video trainings on how to implement everything I'm teaching you, check out our digital training course Ignite here: www.ignitecourse.com

Chapter 6: Mastering Lead Generation

When most people think of building out a marketing strategy, they start with their lead generation strategy and think that is the beginning. By setting your foundation beforehand, you're here with an already clear understanding of your marketing foundation and a plan on how you will connect with your audience using valuable content. Now, you're truly ready to master your lead generation and grow your email list, filled with potential customers.

If you're selling a digital product or service such as coaching or an online course, about eighty percent of your marketing budget is going to be spent driving people to the *top of your funnel* where you will capture their name and email address in exchange for something of value that you're giving away. If you're an ecommerce business selling a physical product you will probably spend more like ten to twenty percent of your budget here gathering email leads onto your newsletter list.

Your lead generation strategy is extremely crucial because it's typically the step right before you make your offer, and you need to position your brand correctly for the offer to convert into sales.

The main goal in the lead generation phase is to create a strategy where people consume the content and make it to your offer. Effective lead generation strategies make sure that once a lead consumes what they signed up for, purchasing your product or service feels like an easy next step to solving their problem.

Choosing Your Lead Generation Strategy

There are many different types of lead generation strategies you can use, and I am going to give you some top converting examples, based on my actual personal experience, as well as experience with our many clients in various industries. As you review the top converting strategies, I want you to remember the importance of customizing your strategy for your audience as well as the persona you've already identified. Make sure whatever you choose to be your lead generation strategy is going to be the most effective way to attract your ideal customer. Consistently revisit the idea that marketing is about a connection, and view your lead generation strategy as another opportunity to connect and build trust with your audience. This will ultimately help them see that your paid offer is exactly what they need next.

It's important not to pick one of my examples or anyone else's strategy for that matter, and replicate it exactly, but instead use one of the examples as a template. You have to remember that your audience and your offer is going to be different than my business or somebody else's business so replicating an exact strategy somebody else is using may not work for your audience or for what you're selling. Instead, put yourself in the shoes of your ideal customer and decide what you need to do to customize it and connect with them in the most effective way. Some proven top converting lead generation strategies we often see are webinars, challenges, video series, quizzes, lead magnets or applications to book a call.

Webinars

Webinars are probably the most common strategy we use with clients, and one of the most effective, because it's one powerful video training that connects people with you for about thirty to sixty minutes, and then pitches them on your offer. Webinars are great for offers over $500, where people most likely need to see and connect with you on video to buy from you.

The content you put in the webinar, the length of it, and the amount of nurturing that happens before and after the webinar are the parts you need to customize based on your audience and the price of your product.

The main goal of a webinar is to *build authority and trust* with your audience. You don't want to teach your audience so much in the webinar that they are overwhelmed and don't feel like they need to buy anything by the end of it. Instead, you want to build authority by using case studies or examples of the results you've been able to deliver for your past customers. You also want to help your audience have epiphanies and realizations throughout your webinar that your brand's expertise and your personal knowledge are the answer to solving their particular problem.

For example, if I was to do a webinar on Facebook ads I wouldn't teach somebody how to actually run an ad or implement a strategy, I would help them see why they haven't gotten the results they wanted to yet. I would use my knowledge and content to *show* them that they are missing components in their marketing strategy instead of giving them every single piece of the *how* to fix it. This will put them in a position by the end of the training where they know my content and expertise is the answer to their problem and hopefully buy my offer.

A great format for your webinar is to teach 3 main secrets or tips and make sure those really hit on solving your ideal customers biggest pain points that you've already identified in Step 1 of *The Hirsh Process.*

Your webinar title and messaging should also focus on your ideal customers biggest pain points so that it draws them in immediately. Some example webinar titles that have worked well for us and our clients are:

"3 Secrets To Exploding Your Brand Without Blowing Up Your Ads Budget -- Using Our Million Dollar Process"

"3 Secrets to Planning, Launching and Growing Your Online Store...even if you aren't sure what to sell yet!"

"How To Build Wealth Without Gambling In The Casino Of Wall Street"

You can find deeper trainings on creating webinars with our webinar strategy training, sample webinar script, sample webinar slides and sample webinar Facebook ads inside Ignite: www.ignitecourse.com

Challenges

Challenges are an excellent live launch or live experience option. They work especially well in the health and fitness industry, or with any audience where they are inspired to make the time to put into going through the challenge experience. Challenges work best when done live and when they last between three to five days. This means the challenge starts and ends on specific dates, and everyone participating goes through it together. This allows the engagement and participation to be powerful, which will help the conversion of the offer that you make at the end of the challenge.

The goal with a challenge is to help people get a micro-result during their experience. After, when they are pitched your offer, it functions as the no-brainer, next step for them. They are going to be inspired to keep going. A word of advice: Be careful not to teach too much in a challenge, because you will leave people overwhelmed and not interested in purchasing from you. Keep it simple!

Some great examples of challenges are clean eating challenges or challenges where you help the participants accomplish something they are struggling with such as posting their first video online, planning their meals or connecting with their partner.

The length of your challenge, the content you create for it, and the time commitment you want out of people during the challenge, will all depend on your audience and what is going to serve them best. When it comes time to pitch your offer towards the end of the challenge, you can choose to add in a webinar or bonus training on the last day, where your offer will be introduced *after* that training. For a challenge to convert, your offer must *relate* to the experience they just went through and is a clear next step for them to get the result they want.

Video Series

Video series are great for live launches and are most commonly paired with a webinar at the end. The most common and effective way to implement a video series is to have people sign up to get access to your video series, have specific dates each video is released, and make the final day a live webinar where the offer is pitched.

My team and I have found that video series doesn't work as well if it's not a live launch with specific release dates because you will lose the audience through the video series and they won't make it to the webinar, which means they don't make it to the important pitch of your offer. When doing these live, it's key that you get some form of engagement from people going through the video series. Strategies we have seen work well are creating a Facebook group for people as they go through the video series, doing bonus Facebook lives for everyone participating to add some extra connection, and providing the audience with a workbook as they go through the content.

The length of your videos, the content in your videos, and how many videos you have, are all things you should decide based on your ideal audience and the product or service you offer. Similar to the challenge, it's crucial you don't teach too much during the video series, leaving your audience overwhelmed. Instead, help them break beliefs or barriers and ultimately see that your offer is the clear next step to solving their problem.

Lead Magnets

Lead magnets are a great way to inexpensively grow your email list because they usually are a low time commitment for the audience. Examples of some converting lead magnets are checklists, blueprints, swipe files, or PDF guides.

The downside with lead magnets is that they are a low commitment for people, which means they don't build as much connection as a live video training or challenge would. If you're trying to grow your list to then eventually launch something, or you're trying to warm people up to get them on a webinar, a lead magnet may be a great option for your strategy. Lead magnets are also great if you're pitching a low-priced offer on the backend, such as a $100 or $200 product that can be pitched through email with only a few touch points beforehand.

If you do choose a lead magnet, make sure you have something you will be offering those leads either right away on the backend, or in the next ninety days. You don't want to grow your list just to see it grow, you want to make sure you're making money back growing your list, and the only way to do that is to have a planned offer to make to these leads.

What lead magnet to choose and the next steps you take to make an offer to those leads in your customer journey should be customized to your audience and your specific offer.

Application To Book A Call

If you're selling a service or program that is high priced, typically above $2,000, you will want to get leads on the phone with you or a sales team to then sell them via the phone.

If this is your strategy, your goal in the lead generation step would be to get applications for an appropriate cost per application. Depending on your business and the type of person you're trying to get on the phone with you or your team you may want to have a filter that accepts or declines applicants based on if they are qualified.

For example, my highest level services I offer in my agency requires that clients are making over $100,000 in annual income and can invest at least $3,000 per month on marketing support. It's not a good use of our time or the applicants time to talk on the phone if they are not yet ready for our services. Therefore, we have qualifiers in our application that send them to our digital course if they are not quite ready for our management services based on their answers. This ensures that my sales team is talking to quality leads and helps us achieve better results.

Customizing Your Strategy

No matter what strategy you choose, make sure that it is the right one for that ideal customer persona we documented earlier on, and make sure it will be the most effective way to lead them to your paid offer next. If you're targeting a very busy entrepreneur with a high ticket $1,997 offer, a challenge is most likely not the right choice. If you're targeting a busy mom who rarely gets any time to herself, a webinar might not be the best choice for her.

The first step to mastering your lead generation is choosing the right option for your audience, not because you saw somebody else do it. We can always come back and change it or test something new, but for now, you need to stick to one strategy and then really customize it for your audience and your offer.

Strategically Driving Traffic to the Top of Your Funnel

Once you choose your strategy and you know how you're going to capture your leads and how you're going to sell to them, you will need to drive traffic to the top of that funnel using ads. The top of your funnel is where you will be capturing the leads – it will be your webinar, your video series, your challenge, or your lead magnet and you'll spend eighty percent of your ad budget here if you're selling a digital product or service and ten to twenty percent of your ad budget here if you're selling a physical product.

Make sure to revisit setting your budget in chapter 4 so that, once you're ready to run ads, you know how many leads you need to hit your sales and the cost per lead you are aiming for. Remember, if you haven't run ads before, you probably guessed these numbers based on averages, but once we have actual data, we can create some more solid projections based on your true numbers. In the beginning, you need to get as many quality leads as you can into your funnel so that you can get as many people to see, hear, and engage with your offer as possible.

Targeting Your Ads to Your Ideal Audience

When running your lead generation ads, you need to create strategic targeting to reach your ideal customers. The best way to start your ads and test different targeting is to go off of Facebook pages they might like.

If you haven't done this yet from the brand awareness and visibility ads, I want you to make a list of twenty pages that your ideal customer might follow. Think about people they might follow, magazines they might like, or companies they would support and follow on Facebook. Make sure to put yourself in their shoes and think of them as regular people. Don't be too literal with this and overthink it.

I sometimes see people make the mistake where they say, "I am targeting business coaches, but I can't find any pages that say 'business coaches to target." Instead of trying to find pages that directly say "business coach," what would be more effective is targeting other large entrepreneurs, such as Marie Forleo or Female Entrepreneur Association, because those are pages that business coaches probably follow. Another example would be if you're targeting people who want to lose weight, you don't have to directly target "weight loss" you could target health interests such as "weight watchers," health magazines, gyms or various fitness influencers people might follow.

If you need help making your list of twenty pages, you can go into your ads manager and find audience insights. If you plug in a page like "entrepreneur" into audience insights on Facebook, it will tell you other pages people in this audience like, to give you some more ideas.

The reason I want you to create a list of twenty page options is that not everyone is going to be targetable on Facebook. Based on the size of the audience and the data Facebook has on the audience, they will either allow you to target the audience or they won't. If you create twenty options, you should be able to target at least half of those.

Once you have your list of audiences, you can start targeting them and testing them with your ads. You're most likely going to find that some audiences convert better than others, and you will then turn off the ones that don't convert and put money into the ones that are converting better.

Testing Your Ads

A massive mistake people make is that they choose about three audiences to test in their campaign and then they stop testing. There are so many options for testing various audiences, and you will probably need to continue to come up with new ones as you keep running your ads. I often look into a campaign that a previous agency ran for our clients and see less than five ad sets of audiences they tested, and know immediately they didn't fully test or optimize the campaign to its full potential.

Don't stop testing various audiences until you get a cost per lead that you're happy with, and even once you get some audiences converting, you can continue to test new ones. We often have client campaigns with 200 or more ad sets inside of them because we are testing so many different ones.

To start, I would take your daily ad budget and divide it by five. Whatever number you get is how many ad sets you can afford to have each day and how many audiences you should test. For example, if your daily ad budget is $50 you can have ten different ad set to $5 per day budget, all testing different audience options.

We will talk later about troubleshooting and optimizing your ads if they aren't converting, but also keep in mind that a very important piece of your lead generation strategy is going to be the *actual messaging* in your ads. You should be testing your audiences as well as your ad creative. Test long ad copy, short ad copy, images with and without text, video ads, GIF ads, and boomerang ads. You don't know what will convert with your audience until you try it, and one or two versions of creative are not enough to decide. There is no cookie statement such as "video ads always do better than images." It depends on your audience and brand and that's why it's important to always be testing the various options against each other.

Our team typically uses what we call *the sandbox technique* when testing new ad creative. We start with three to four different versions of creative, and we first test the headlines using plain lifestyle images with no text. We then take those winning headlines and test various images with the winning headlines. This allows us to know what our winning headline is and then what our winning image is, and, finally, we can test various body copy in the ads such as long copy versus short copy. Notice how when we are in a strong testing phase, we are looking at one factor at a time, instead of changing a bunch of things at once, which wouldn't allow us to narrow down what is and isn't working.

Once you have an audience or an ad creative version

that is working, then you don't want to turn it off to keep testing. Keep what is working on, turn off what isn't working, and replace what isn't working with either new audiences or new creative. If you don't do the work to test various audience options, as well as various ad creative, you are throwing money away. If you get to a $4 cost per lead and just settle without doing enough testing and variation, you could be settling for a $4 cost per lead, when it's possible to get it to $3, or maybe even less.

The actual process of testing your ads and nailing the audiences, copy, and creative can be very overwhelming. If you want more customized help with this in your business, we have a very in-depth digital course and coaching program that does just that. You can learn more about it here: www.ignitecourse.com

Using Facebook Data Strategically

When you first start with Facebook ads, you don't have a lot of data in your ad account. However, as soon as you start running either brand awareness ads or lead generation ads, you're not only getting leads and followers, but you're also getting data.

The data you gather within your Facebook ad account is one of the most valuable things about Facebook marketing and should be used strategically. You can use this data as specific audiences you create within your ads account, and you can also turn those audiences into what's called "lookalike audiences."

Lookalike audiences are you telling Facebook, "Here is a base audience of people that I know are my ideal customer. Find me one to ten million more of those people that I can target my ads to." Most of the time, these looka-like audiences convert better than the audiences you choose based on interests, because the reality is, Face-book knows its users better than we do, and the data it has on users is extremely powerful.

Once you begin running ads, you should use the data strategically for your targeting in the lead generation phase. Some examples of common audiences you can use for both retargeting your audiences and lookalike audiences are:

Retargeting audiences:
- 25 percent video viewers of your videos you post on your business page

- 50 percent video viewers of your videos you post on your business page

- 75 percent video viewers of your videos you post on your business page

- 90 percent video viewers of your videos you post on your business page

- Website traffic in the last 180 days

- Website traffic to your podcast pages in the last 180 days

- Website traffic to your blog in the last 180 days

- Facebook page engagement

Lookalike audiences you can use:
- 1 percent and 2 percent lookalike audiences of your 50 percent video viewers

- 1 percent and 2 percent lookalike audiences of your 75 percent video viewers
- 1 percent and 2 percent lookalike audiences of your 90 percent video viewers
- 1 percent and 2 percent lookalike audience of your website traffic
- 1 percent and 2 percent lookalike of your podcast or blog traffic
- 1 percent and 2 percent lookalike of your Facebook page engagement
- 1 percent and 2 percent lookalike of people who have visited your landing page to the top of your funnel
- 1 percent and 2 percent lookalike of people who have signed up with their email address to the top of your funnel
- 1 percent and 2 percent lookalike of your buyers (once you have 100)

The retargeted audiences would be targeting the warm traffic that you built from your brand awareness and visibility content phase. This audience has already had a touchpoint with your brand, and you want them to take the next step in your customer journey, which is usually to take the first step in your customer journey. Keep in mind when targeting this audience that they have already had the touchpoint with your brand, and you can address this strategically in the ad copy.

For example, if you're targeting your video view

audiences, then you know they are interested in your video content, and you can reference that in your ad copy. Coming back to that idea of connection, use that information you have to connect with your audience, which will ultimately help your ads stand out and convert better.

The lookalike audiences will be cold traffic, people who have not had any touch points with your brand previously. These audiences are used in conjunction with the interest-based audiences you listed at the beginning of this chapter as an audience to test. We often find lookalike audiences convert the best for our clients because the data Facebook has on its users is just more powerful than anything we could manually target, but you won't know what converts for you until you test it.

Fully Mastering Your Lead Generation

Running ads to the top of your funnel can be overwhelming because it's where most of your budget goes and it's one of the most important pieces of your overall marketing strategy. To have success, you need to get as many quality leads as possible so you can get as many sales as possible.

The keys to truly mastering your lead generation without the overwhelm, is first creating a strategy that is based around connecting with your ideal customer and will accomplish the job of attracting them and converting them to buyers. Next, make sure you understand your numbers and budget from the beginning. There shouldn't be any guesses or surprises in this phase. You should know *exactly* how many leads you are aiming to get and how much you want to be paying for each one.

Then, look at testing your audiences and ads, as if you're a research scientist trying to narrow down what is and isn't working. It's crucial you do enough testing and don't stop at only a few audiences and a few ad creative versions. Finally, make sure you use the data you're gathering in your ad account for both warm and cold traffic targeting. You will spend a lot of your budget and a lot of your time here, and it might take you some time to truly master your lead generation. But once you do, you will have unlocked one of the hardest pieces of your marketing strategy and everything else will feel easier.

It's really easy to get overwhelmed and emotional if your lead generation is not converting into leads, or your leads aren't converting to sales. This is often the phase where people give up on their ads and marketing and restart everything. Following the process laid out in this chapter will help you stay logical and help you to look at everything as numbers and data. Having this mindset, you will be so much more effective at troubleshooting and optimizing your ads as you go.

Chapter 7: Make Money and Master Retargeting

Once you're strategically growing your brand and following with valuable content, and bringing leads into the top of your funnel to sell to them, you can focus on the sales and retargeting of all of those leads using very strategic follow-ups. At this phase, your main goal is to successfully convert the leads that you've connected with, and most likely paid to get onto your email list, to become a paying customer. If you are selling a physical product, eighty percent of your ad budget will go to this step and if you're selling a digital product or service about ten percent of your ad budget will go to this step.

At some point in your lead generation process, you should have already made your offer to people. After you make your offer, you have a promotional window where, during that time, your goal is to get those leads to buy from you. Whether you made your offer on a webinar, during your challenge, or at the end of your video series, you're now left with extremely hot leads that you need to build trust with and hopefully convince them to purchase your offer. Your main goal here is to connect with these hot leads and help them realize that your offer is the answer to solving their problem and changing their life. And of course, you need to believe that this is true!

Many people feel like selling feels scam-y or gross, and they tend to hide when it comes time to make the sale. Instead of seeing sales as pushy or scam-y, I want you to view it as serving your audience with exactly what you know they need. You would be doing them a disservice not selling what you have to offer because you know it's going to make such a difference in their lives. The difference between you and the people who are scam-y with their sales is that you have constantly prioritized value and trust while building this audience. You have also worked hard to successfully attract the exact ideal customer because you know what that person needs on a deep level. You know who this person is, and you already know they need what you have to offer. When you sell from a place of serving this ideal person that you've been speaking to and attracting all this time, you're easily able to feel how selling is just connecting and serving, and it shouldn't feel overly pushy or uncomfortable.

Core Components to Successfully Selling

To have a successful offer in your funnel, you must have follow-ups after you initially make your offer. There will be a small percentage of your audience that will buy right away after hearing it, and then you will have another percentage of people who take time to make decisions and will buy after they hear your offer a few times and have considered it. If you don't have effective follow-ups in place after initially making your offer, you may lose all of those people who are on the fence. Those follow-ups should consist of emails, social media posts, videos, and retargeted ads.

In all of your follow-ups, whether they are ads or emails, you have to make sure you are still connecting with your audience. Don't lose that connection and emotion just because it's time to sell. You can connect with your audience by treating your sales language as a story, and even giving some value in the message. For example, if you're writing an email, don't just tell people about the offer and tell them to go and buy it, tell a story about why you created the offer, or maybe a story about somebody who has had success from your offer in the past. Bring out emotion and connection in all of your sales language, and selling will feel easy.

You also must have real urgency in your follow-up. If you make an offer and tell people they can buy whenever, you're leaving it up to them to remember, and leaving it up to them to decide whether they will buy later on or now. You will lose people doing this. I've talked to many people who feel uncomfortable with urgency because they think it feels scam-y, but it's one of those things that just works. You will see more success using it than if you don't. Human beings make decisions a lot faster if they have a deadline – it's just a fact of psychology. By utilizing urgency you're also motivating your potential customers to take action when they may be holding themselves back from something they deeply want. You don't have to fake urgency. It's obvious when urgency is being faked, and I suggest you have authentic urgency. You don't want to lie to people, because that will lose their trust and that is the opposite of what I've been discussing with you this entire time. Some great examples of urgency are your price going up after a certain amount of time, the doors to enrollment closing on a certain date, a bonus going away after a certain date, or having limited spots that you stop selling once they fill up. These are all ways you can create *authentic* urgency, and, therefore, encourage people to take action much faster.

General Sales Ads

If you have a physical products business a lot of this step will be spent running general sales ads to purchase your product or products. You will most likely spend eighty percent of your ad budget running these sales ads.

Wherever you're sending people from your ad, it's important that it's very clear what action they should take. If you send people from an ad to a website page with ten to twenty different product options to purchase, you're most likely going to overwhelm them and they won't end up buying anything.

Instead, create a customer journey where you send people from an ad to one of your top selling or core products and then maybe after they buy that you offer them additional products as *upsells,* is a lot more effective. The key is that you still create a *journey* for your potential customers to go through that clearly lays out what to buy.

One of the biggest contributing factors to success with our e-commerce clients has been really innovative creative used in the ads themselves. When driving traffic from a Facebook ad directly to a product a lot of the selling has to happen in the ad itself. Using strategic videos, boomerangs, GIFs, images and ad copy will capture people's attention and get them intrigued by what you have to offer.

Using Retargeted Ads to Close More Sales

Many people build out a customer journey with follow-up emails but don't create retargeted ads. If you're doing this, you're leaving money on the table. Retargeted ads are often more effective than email because people will see them more than they will read their email. Your goal at this phase of your customer journey is to be visible everywhere and to continually remind people of the amazing offer you have and the limited time they have to take advantage of it.

The best way to strategize your retargeting ads is to physically draw out your customer journey and then pair a retargeting ad at every step you want someone to take action. If you've spent money on your lead generation phase, you already have a handful of audiences you can retarget simply by driving traffic through your funnel. These people are also very inexpensive to reach because they are hyper-targeted audiences.

An example of a common retargeted ad is if you're running traffic to a webinar and after the webinar, the leads have five days to enroll in your course before the price goes up. You would show them retargeted ads for those five days to communicate this to them. This example would be general retargeting ads that are targeting a large group of your warm audience. Having general retargeting ads is level one. Level two is a process of getting very specific with your retargeting ads.

One of the differences of Facebook compared to other advertising platforms is how specific you can get with your audiences and retargeting. With Facebook audiences, you are able target people who have taken specific actions, such as watching your webinar, landing on your sales page before, or have maybe even gotten to your checkout page but didn't buy yet. They are some of the most effective and cheap ads you can run.

Ads for People Who Did *Not* Watch Your Webinar

Your webinar is going to be the most effective way you can get people to become a buyer. The people who watch your webinar are far more likely to purchase your offer. If you run traffic to a webinar, you most likely have a whole audience of people who have signed up but not watched yet. Using either the pixel or an email list of people, you can create an audience who have signed up for your webinar but not watched it yet, and send them back to watch the webinar.

I recommend doing this for the first twenty-four hours after your webinar and creating a specific ad that acknowledges they signed up for the webinar and can still watch it by clicking on that ad. The ad will then take them directly to your webinar replay.

Ads for People Who *Did* Watch Your Webinar

You have an even warmer audience of people who did watch your webinar and didn't buy, and you can create a specific ad for them that talks directly about the webinar and how the offer you pitched on the webinar is exactly what they need next. By speaking to these people directly, you can connect on a whole different level than a general retargeting ad would. I would consider making a video here speaking directly to these people, telling them how much fun you had on the webinar and how you can't wait for them to sign up for your offer.

Final Twenty-Four Hours Ad

Whatever the last twenty-four hours of your urgency are, you can run an ad speaking to this and show it to all of the people who haven't purchased yet. This is a standard ad we run for our clients and it communicates the message that the audience has a limited time left before either the cart closes, the price goes up, or the bonus disappears. The copy in this ad should specifically acknowledge the urgency and get people to take action.

Ads for People Who Have Visited Your Sales Page or Checkout Page

Abandoned sales page and abandoned cart ads are my favorite because of how effective and easy they are. In one of our larger client launches, they spent $1,100 on an abandon cart ad and made back $1.1M in sales. By the way, that was *not* a typo, those are real results! These ads are so effective because you're talking to the *hottest* audience you have, people who are right on the fence. They want to buy, but for whatever reason, haven't yet. You will see companies like Amazon show these ads on products you looked at all the time. However, if you're an *influencer* or the face of a brand, using a video is an even more effective way to create these ads.

That client that got over 10,000 percent return on her ad spend with this ad created a straight-to-camera video that was less than one minute, and directly acknowledged she knew they were on the fence, but here's why they should buy and she couldn't wait to see them in her program.

I'll say it again: *marketing is a connection.* This type of ad is the ultimate form of connection that will get people's attention and convince them to make the jump and invest in your offer.

Dynamic Retargeting Ads

Dynamic retargeting ads are a must for anyone selling multiple physical products in a store. Dynamic ads can be set up typically using your storefront, like Shopify, and connecting it to your Facebook ads account. These ads will then automatically show to people who have checked out a product on your site but have not purchased it yet.

You'll see ads from Amazon that do this all the time if you view a product and don't finish buying it. The power behind dynamic retargeting ads is they will send people back to a product they showed interest in after viewing it and not purchasing.

The Best Return On Your Ad Spend You Can Have

You've spent a lot of effort and money to get leads interested in what you have to sell, now it's time to add the icing on the cake and make sure that a high percentage of those leads become bonafide sales. Retargeting ads and strategic follow-ups will do exactly that. And even more good news, they are extremely cost-effective.

It doesn't matter if you're running ads that are always on, or running ads that are for a live launch happening on specific dates. Either way, you can and should have strategic retargeted ads. If you're able to create ads that are specific to the audience and connect with them based on where they are in your customer journey, you will see a massive improvement in your overall results and and a return on your ad spend investment.

Congratulations! At this point, you now have a full marketing strategy and customer journey that should successfully attract buyers and grow your business and sales! Next, it's time to analyze your strategy and decide what is and isn't working, so that you can either optimize and fix it, or scale it to get even better results.

Chapter 8: Marketing Is Numbers

As soon as you start spending money on your paid traffic, you're buying data, and you're able to take those numbers and make decisions based off of them. At this point in the process, you have a marketing strategy that was created and customized, specific to your ideal customer. Once your lead generation ads are set up, you'll be driving as many people as possible into your funnel and gathering information as they come in.

The next step is an ongoing step that will never be completed. As long as you're running paid ads, you'll be gathering data where you need to review numbers and make decisions around them. There are two ways I like to look at data depending, on if you've run ads before or you haven't.

Buying Data

If you've never run ads before or you're running ads to a brand-new funnel, you're in what I call a *buying data phase*. This means you're paying to get people into your funnel just to get the data. Your funnel is most likely not perfect and will have holes in it, but your main priority is to get at least one hundred people into the funnel so that you can see what happens once they are in. You're paying for ads to get people into the funnel knowing that what you have is not perfect, but also know that unless you get people in the funnel, you're not going to know what to fix.

Once you begin buying data, you're watching for these type of metrics:

- What percentage of people signed up with their name and email that landed on your registration page or landing page? This is your landing page conversion.

- What percentage of people came to your live webinar? This is your webinar show up rate.

- What percentage of people participated in your challenge or watched your video series? This is your participation rate.

- What percentage of people opened your emails? This is your email open rate.

- What percentage of people that signed up bought your offer? This is your sales conversion.

- How much did you spend and how much did you make? This is your retrun on ad spend or ROAs.

If you can get the answer to these questions through real numbers, you will quickly know what the issues are and what you need to fix to have a converting strategy.

People often think that when they start to run paid ads, they will make their money back almost immediately, and if they don't start making money back almost immediately, then they are frustrated and feel like nothing is working for them and they want to quit and restart.

I want you to change your perspective on paid ads. Just like how growing your following and business is about the long game, so are paid ads and marketing. Mastering a marketing strategy is an investment, and it often takes time to get it to convert. This is completely normal and it's how it works for most companies – even the ones you see making millions of dollars go through this phase.

When you're marketing a new funnel, your number one priority is to *buy data*. My suggestion is you commit to a monthly budget, using the budget planning taught in chapter 4. If it's possible, I would spend at least $500-$1,000 a month, so you can get enough traffic into your funnel to analyze it. Based on averages, you can calculate an estimate on what results you will get from that budget. However, you also need to be willing and okay with *not* making that money back in the first thirty to ninety days. *When* you start making money back will depend on how long it's going to take you to optimize your strategy and get it converting. For some, it takes as little as two weeks until they are making a profit, but for most of you, it will take up to ninety days. It will take even longer if you're not driving enough people into your funnel to get data.

If you're in this phase, I want you to look at your marketing ad spend as an *investment* instead of an expense. You're *investing* in getting traffic to your brand and into your funnel so that you can fine-tune your strategy and your messaging to convert. If you're willing to make that investment and come out on the other side with a strategy that spits out $3 for every $1 you spend, it may end up being the best investment you ever make.

Analyzing An Already Converting Strategy

If you have a funnel or a marketing strategy that you know already converts because you've run paid traffic to it in the past, then you probably don't have to buy data because you already have the data on how it converts. People in this category will take the previous data they have, use that to create projections for their leads, sales, and ad spend, and then track against those projections. If your funnel and strategy converts the way it did before, then making a profit should happen almost immediately because your projections should come close to matching your results.

If for some reason you start running ads and they are not converting as they did before, then you will want to look at any factor you've changed that could cause that to happen. Sometimes, when a lot of time has passed, an industry can change, and projections might have to be readjusted based on a new normal. For example, as the online coaching space has gotten more saturated, the cost to advertise has gotten more expensive and we've seen an increase in cost per results. However, if you've changed pieces of your strategy since the last time you had this data, you will want to look at that and see if you need to change something back.

What Numbers to Track

There are consistent metrics you want to always be tracking so that you're able to analyze and look at a strategy to find holes. I recommend tracking these numbers daily in a spreadsheet and then analyzing your weekly and monthly averages to look for trends or big changes from one week or month to the next. Some of these numbers are specific to certain types of funnels, so if the metric doesn't apply to your strategy, don't try to track it, but these are the numbers you probably want to track:

- Cost per lead
- Your landing page conversion percentage (number of clicks to your landing page divided by the number of conversions you got)
- Your email open rates after they opt-in
- Your webinar live show-up rate (how many people that signed up are watching your webinar)
- Your sales conversion percentage (how many people that are signing up at the top of your funnel are buying your offer)
- Your cost per application (if you have something high ticket where you're trying to get people on the phone, how much each of those phone calls are costing)
- Your return on investment or ROI (how much are you spending and how much are you making back)

To get access to exclusive Hirsh Marketing's ad tracking spreadsheet that you can use and customize for your business, download it here: www.hmadtracking.com

Making Decisions With Your Numbers

Once you start tracking these numbers, you have data that you can use to figure out where there might be holes in your funnel and what needs to be fixed to get it to convert. My suggestion is to go through the list from top to bottom and stop when you find the first issue. For example, if you have a high cost per lead and you're not getting enough people in your funnel, it's going to impact every other metric after that. Fix the high cost per lead first and then move on to the next issue down the funnel.

It's also important you focus on fixing one piece at a time. If you try to fix your ads, your funnel, and your offer positioning all at once, you're not going to know what is and isn't working, because it could be any one of these elements. Let's look at what to do with the various issues you might find in your funnel.

My Cost Per Lead Is High

If your cost per lead or cost per click on your ad is high, you need to work on the ad itself. There are two main factors that can cause a high ad cost, and that's your targeting or your messaging. More times than not, it's the messaging, so if this is what you're struggling with, your next step is to look at your ad creative and messaging and see how it can be improved. Can you go deeper with your messaging to connect emotionally with your audience? Are you talking to your ideal customer in a way that is going to get them to stop scrolling and take action? Are you truly communicating the benefit they will get, by signing up for and clicking on what you're offering them?

If it's not the messaging, then it's probably the targeting. Evaluate your targeting and see if it needs some fine-tuning. Are you for sure targeting audiences where your ideal customer is going to be? Can you come up with some different audiences to test and compare that with what you've tried so far?

Make the changes to either your messaging or your targeting and then test again. See if your cost per lead goes down.

My Landing Page Is Not Converting

If you're getting clicks from your ad but less than 25 to 30 percent of people aren't signing up, you have a landing page issue. Most of the time when this happens, the landing page is either not clear or there is a disconnect with the people you're getting to click on the ad. They are either confused or don't want what you're asking them to sign up for.

To troubleshoot this, put yourself in the shoes of the person clicking on the ad, and make sure it makes sense when they get to the landing page. Was it cohesive and does it seem like a logical next step to sign up, based on what your ad said? Also, check to make sure that your targeting strategy is attracting quality people, not just people who are going to click on an ad and bounce.

Another common issue with landing pages is that they aren't made mobile-friendly enough, or the sign-up button is unclear or hidden. This can greatly affect your conversions, so make sure your page is mobile-friendly and your sign-up button is towards the top of the page and easy to find.

My Email Open Rates Are Low

If nobody is opening your emails after they opt in to your funnel, then you either are getting poor quality leads, have an email deliverability issue, or your subject lines are not strong enough. The first step is to make sure you don't have an email deliverability issue, which you can usually check by talking to your email service provider. If you don't, then make sure your targeting is not off and you're getting the right people into your funnel.

If those two things are not the issue, then start testing some more engaging subject lines. Remember to look at your funnel from the perspective of your ideal customer and ask yourself, "What headline would get them to be interested enough to open the email?"

My Webinar Show-Up Rate Is Low

If nobody comes to your webinar after signing up, then they aren't hearing your offer and therefore will have a hard time converting to a paid customer. Factors to look at if nobody is coming to your webinar is the time of the webinar if you're running it live, making sure you have enough reminder emails set up so people remember to come, confirming that it's easy to access the webinar and doesn't have a bunch of hoops for somebody to jump through, and possibly creating an extra incentive for people to come live. If you're running a live webinar at a specific date and time, you might need to play with some different times of day and days of the week to see which one your audience is most responsive to.

Check your funnel and make sure you have three to

four reminder emails set up for in-between when somebody signs up for the webinar and the webinar happens. People don't always remember what they signed up for, and it's your job to remind them and make sure they know how important this training is for them to attend. Don't assume they are going to just set aside time and come to your webinar. Make them understand how life-changing coming to your webinar is going to be for them. It doesn't matter if you're running a live or an ongoing evergreen webinar, you need solid reminder emails so people know where to go and why they should attend. Go through your funnel process and put yourself in the shoes of your audience. Is it easy to find your webinar and access it? If there are tech hoops they have to jump through or they are not clear where to go, you will lose people.

If you're struggling to get people to come to the live, you can offer an incentive for everyone who attends. We've seen this work many times, using either a giveaway such as a free ticket to your event, or a free strategy call with you. You can also give away something like a bonus resource, where you only share the link to access it on the webinar for people who are there live. If you choose to use this strategy, you have to make sure people know about this incentive right after they sign up for your webinar on the thank you page, as well as in all of your reminder emails. I would not recommend giving away something like an iPad or headphones, because then you're going to get people who only care about that giveaway and don't care at all about your content. Make the giveaway relevant to your content and the problem your company solves for people so that it still attracts the right person to attend your webinar.

Another effective strategy to help your webinar attendance rate is to make sure your webinar thank you page has some strategic reminders on it. If you're doing a live webinar, you can create a Google Calendar link, where people can click it and add the webinar to their calendar. You can also use tools like *Manychat* to have them click a button and get a reminder via Facebook messenger as to when your webinar is happening.

To get as many people live on your webinar as possible, you need to effectively remind them that it's happening, make it easy for them to attend and find the webinar link, and also communicate very clearly and effectively all of the reasons this free training will support them.

My Offer Is Not Converting In My Funnel

An offer not converting to sales in your funnel is a very common issue people have because making a sale is not always easy. If you're getting leads into your funnel, they are consuming your content by opening your emails and attending your webinar, but then, when it comes time to buy your offer, they are not buying, it's most likely the positioning of your offer. If they are making it as far as watching your webinar and hearing your offer, but then not buying, they are most likely your ideal audience because they made it that far. If this is happening, there is probably a gap in the way your offer has been positioned or the way you've set them up to hear the offer.

The first step is to look at the messaging in your actual offer. Does it communicate the problem you will solve for your audience and the benefits of signing up for what you're offering? Oftentimes, people focus on all of the features or pieces of their offer, instead of the benefits of the offer itself. Your audience doesn't care how they are going to achieve something, they care what achieving it is going to do for them. Your offer needs to communicate the results somebody will have by signing up for it.

Messaging and positioning can take time to test, which is why if you have a new funnel, you're buying data to get people in the funnel and testing the positioning of your offer. As you look at optimizing the messaging of your offer, put yourself in the position of your ideal customer and ask yourself, "Is the offer clear?" "Are the benefits of buying the offer communicated?" "Would I buy this?"

Once you look at the messaging in your offer, you can make sure you have all of the proper follow-ups in place, so that people are being reminded to buy and it's also communicated why this offer is exactly what they need. Check to make sure you have enough follow-up emails after you're pitching the offer, as well as retargeting ads set up. These touchpoints will help you stay top of mind during your promotional window while you're trying to get sales.

We talked about this in the previous chapter, but make sure you also have a sense of urgency communicated in your offer. If your audience has no reason to decide, they will most likely wait or forget to make a decision at all. Authentic urgency will help encourage your audience to take action instead of waiting.

Once you look at the offer itself and make sure the messaging and strategy is effective, you might need to look at how people are being guided up until the point of your offer. Oftentimes, people teach so much in their webinar or their challenge that they overwhelm the audience and leave them paralyzed when it comes time to buy. You're an expert in what you teach, so you're probably going to want to teach way more than people need because you will think the basics are not enough. Your job between when somebody enters your funnel and when they are pitched the offer is to give value, but to not over-teach. Rather than giving them the exact steps to go and accomplish a result, your content should help people change their beliefs about something, or see that what they thought was impossible is actually possible. Your content leading up to the offer should be showing people the *what* and your offer is the *how*. If you set it up correctly, when they get to your offer, the offer will feel required to achieve the result they want.

Nailing down your offer and getting your sales conversions to where you want them is probably one of the hardest components to a converting strategy, and often it takes time and testing. Everything else in the funnel before this must be converting so that people get to hear your offer. If it's converting, then it's time to truly perfect your offer. Analyze the messaging, make sure there is authentic urgency, and make sure your content is setting you up for success when the time comes to pitch your offer.

Marketing *Always* Works

You'll often hear me say:

"Marketing *always* works; it's just a matter of *when*."

I say this because if you're willing to stick to the

process laid out above, where you put people through your funnel, look at the data, and stop at each hole in order to repair it and then repeat the process until it's converting, your marketing *will work*. There is no way you can fail doing this, it just might take you a few months. The mistake people make is they go through this process for a short period, and then give up and create a brand-new funnel, which puts them back at square one. The answer to a struggling funnel is usually not to create a new and different funnel, it's to fix the struggling funnel.

There are some cases where the offer is just not what people want, or the funnel really is not the right option for their audience, but if you did the work in chapter 4, where we tuned in to your ideal customer persona and clearly defined who they were and the problem you solve, your offer and funnel should be right for your audience. Now it's a matter of optimizing it until it works.

Optimizing Versus Scaling

Everything that we went through so far in this chapter is centered around optimizing a funnel. Optimizing a funnel means you're analyzing the numbers and fixing the holes until it's making you money. Optimizing can take a few months, but once your funnel is optimized and profitable, you're ready to scale. Scaling means adding more money to your ad spend to make more money on the backend. Your ultimate goal with a marketing strategy is to know exactly how much money you make for everything you spend. If you can consistently make $2, $3, $4, $5, for every $1 you spend, then you have just created the most profitable investment you will ever have.

Remember how I said buying data and trusting this process, even if it means it's an expense for a few months, is worth it? This is why. On the other side of that process is an ATM you just created in your business that is extremely profitable. That's your ultimate goal and once you get here, you're ready to spend more money.

I often see people who have a profitable funnel but don't know their numbers, so they don't increase their ad spend. When I ask why this is, they never know, besides not realizing their numbers and the potential they are sitting on. It's crucial to know your numbers when you're scaling because you need to be able to justify increasing your ad spend budget to make even more money on the backend. Wouldn't you rather spend $5,000 to make $15,000 then spend $2,000 to make $6,000?

When it's time to scale you will scale about thirty percent every week, and watch your numbers as you do it. Sometimes, if you scale too quickly with Facebook ads, it throws off the algorithm and increases the cost, so you need to let it settle before adding more budget. Set goals for scaling, just like you set goals for achieving various numbers in your funnel, and then track your progress.

Scaling has a lot of details to it and can be overwhelming to make decisions about what audiences to add in, how often to create new ads, how much budget to increase and when to turn things off. Scaling is very complex and my team and I offer in-depth video trainings and live coaching around this in our program Ignite which you can get access to here: www.ignitecourse.com

Marketing Is Just Numbers

When you decide to change or alter any strategy, you should be choosing to do so based on real data telling you that you should. The tracking I laid out above will tell you exactly what you need to fix in your funnel and strategy. If you're making decisions based on these numbers, you will be moving towards a converting funnel much faster. If you're making decisions because of emotions or fear of things not working, you are making the process a lot harder and longer.

I've had to coach many clients through wanting to completely change their strategy because they think what they have is not working. I know that spending money on your ads can be scary and emotional, and I know that sometimes when something isn't working, you want to throw everything away, instead of fixing the pieces of what's not working. I've been there myself, but you mustn't do that because it will slow down your progress and leave you even more frustrated.

As long as you truly understand your ideal audience and the problem you're solving for them, you will be able to fully make decisions that are driven by numbers. Committing to this way of thinking and this process will help you achieve success much faster than just reacting to your results.

Chapter 9: Mistakes To Watch Out For

One of my favorite parts about being behind the scenes of millions of dollars of ad spend is taking all of that intel and data and finding common themes and mistakes people make when creating and running a paid marketing strategy. Over the last four years, I have found that there are certain pieces to a marketing strategy that are crucial to everyone, regardless of what level they are at in their business or who their audience is.

Paying attention to these common mistakes, and making sure you're not making the same mistakes, will help you achieve success faster without wasting time and money.

Not Prioritizing Value

Over the last few years, there have been a few successful marketers out there who promoted the idea that all you have to do is get one funnel up and running, and you will make tons of money online. This idea has set a lot of people up for frustration and failure because it's simply not realistic. This approach has also saturated the market with people who don't care about building an audience, impacting the world, or delivering value, but instead are just trying to get their one funnel to make money however they can.

There are a few people I've watched have success

with one funnel and pop up online advertising themselves as a "million-dollar company," and then, not long after, collapse and disappear as if they never existed in the first place. Their marketing strategy may have been strong enough in the beginning to bring them temporary success, but they didn't build a loyal following, and they probably didn't deliver on what they were selling, so people did not become loyal to their brand. Sustainable and long-term marketing only works if you're committed to value, both in *building* your audience and on *delivering* your offer once it sells. One of the top factors I attribute my business growth to is constantly focusing on our client delivery. You can't market a product or service that doesn't deliver for long, and you will eventually start to lose a lot of money if you don't focus on your delivery. To create a converting funnel, marketing strategy, and sustainable business that will be known for decades, you have to prioritize value and connecting with your audience.

If you're committed to delivering value and connecting with your audience, you're setting a foundation for a company and brand that will be successful for a long time. Not prioritizing value will result in a slow and painful journey of trying to grow an audience of true believers and not seeing much momentum. This one component is often the key to an entrepreneurs business growth and success but it's not always talked about or visible from the outside. Don't be fooled by shiny object syndrome, where it might look like success and business-growth happens overnight and requires very little work. Building a successful and profitable brand is going to require you to consistently deliver value to your audience and build those loyal followers that will stick by you forever. If you can build an audience of loyal followers, selling and business growth will become extremely easy and effortless. Master this and you'll master your growth.

The Importance Of Focus

When you're starting, you must focus on one funnel, one strategy and one offer. It might seem exciting to have multiple funnels or even sound cool, but it will be detrimental to your success. Everything we've talked about so far about perfecting your messaging, creating a converting strategy, nailing your offer, and then analyzing all the data, has to be done for *every* funnel you create. You can't go through this process with multiple funnels at one time.

If you're trying to perfect multiple funnels, you're going to be spreading not only your time out way too thin, but you're also spreading your ad budget out across multiple funnels. It's much more powerful to put all of your time and energy, as well as budget, into one funnel and make that the best converting funnel possible. After going through this process and all of the steps you must take to achieve a converting strategy and funnel, you can probably see how much work it is to get your funnel converting. Why would you choose to multiply that work by two or even three? It's setting yourself up for failure.

Lacking focus is probably the most common mistake I see in myself, our clients, our students, and, honestly, most entrepreneurs. Many entrepreneurs have the drive to do everything and want to push themselves to a state of slight overwhelm to feel satisfied. I understand this feeling, but trust me, doing multiple things halfway is so much less effective than doing one thing efficiently and strategically.

The two main scenarios where I see people lose focus is when they are starting, as well as when they are already experiencing some success and think they have made it and it's time to create something new.

Losing Focus When You're Starting

When people are starting, they have a lot of ideas circling their heads about strategies they could do and strategies they may have seen others do. It's common to not pick one but to pick multiple and make the mistake of spreading their resources out across multiple strategies and ultimately not having success with any. Go through the process we've talked about and keeping your audience and your offer in mind, and choose the strategy that is the best fit for your business. One strategy. One funnel. One offer. Focus all of your time and money into that funnel until it's that ATM and you're scaling it to the multiple seven-figures.

You might have multiple offers you can sell. I want you to choose one to perfect and focus all your attention on. I know it's tempting to think you should have multiple streams of income, and I am sure they are all great offers. However, it's hard to perfect and optimize one offer, so don't try and perfect two or more offers at once. If you're having trouble choosing your specific offer, think about what you want your core offer to be for your audience. What is going to solve their problem best? What do they need the most or what do you think they will want the most? Your other offers might serve in the future as something you can upsell or down-sell to people who don't buy your core offer, but for now, choose one offer and create a funnel selling that.

Losing Focus Once You're Seeing Success

Losing focus once something is starting to convert or has converted in the past, and you think you've achieved success, is something that I'm even guilty of doing. It's easy to feel like you got this one offer and the funnel is converting, it's making some money, and that now it must be time to create something new and put your focus into that. Don't make this mistake!

Getting your offer or funnel to convert and start making money is just the beginning. Now you have to scale it. Scaling it takes focus because you will need to go through the process of looking at your numbers, adding a budget, and seeing if you can update or improve anything else in your funnel to get even better conversions, to truly get this offer so it's making millions of dollars. If you go and create a new funnel or new offer, you will again be spreading your time and money too thin. Think about how much more effective and powerful it will be to put your time and money into what you already worked so hard to make profitable, and get it converting even better and making even more money. It's not always the most exciting thing to stay focused on one funnel and one offer, especially once you feel like it's working, but it's the most impactful and effective way to grow your company to seven figures and beyond.

It's also really common to want to change your strategy once you have success, just because you think people might get bored with it or maybe *you're* bored with it. I once had a client come to our meeting after a seven-figure launch, and ask me if he should change his whole next launch from a webinar to a challenge. He had just made seven figures with a webinar that was now proven with data we could count on for next time, and we could confidently increase his budget based on the data we had. If we would have changed his strategy to a challenge, it would have been a completely unknown strategy and we would not have been able to confidently spend more money on the next launch. Not to mention, it would be a huge risk because what if the challenge didn't convert the same way the webinar did? We didn't change his strategy, he thankfully listened to me, and we were able to increase his budget by fifty percent the following launch and he more than doubled his sales.

It's not time to create a new funnel or a new offer until your existing offer is making seven figures and you have a team running both the marketing and the delivery of the offer. Once you are in that situation, you will have both the time to work on a new offer yourself, as well as profit coming in from the other funnel, so it can fund step one of getting your new offer to convert, buying data.

If you choose to eventually create a new funnel or offer, you should create one that serves the same audience that your existing, successful offer serves. Don't start a new business and target a brand-new audience. Instead, create an offer that can serve a different level of your existing audience you're already having success with.

The Myth of the Value Ladder

The concept that you must fill a value ladder with offerings for your audience is something I believe sabotages people's focus. A completed value ladder means you have offerings ranging from $40-$3,000 and above to serve your audience at the various levels they might be at. This means if somebody can't afford your $1,000 course, you have something lower priced you can offer them. Or, if somebody bought your $1,000 course, you have something to offer them next. The concept of a value ladder is great in theory, but it's not something you should strive for right out the gate, or even in your first few years of business.

It's a great goal to achieve in the long term of your business, but it should take years to fill your value ladder, and you may never fill it. It's a huge mistake to think that you must have something to offer every lead that comes into your business to be successful. Creating a new offer is not as simple as just selling it to the leads you already have coming in. Creating a new offer will require perfecting the messaging around the offer, creating a strategy to sell it, and then optimizing both the messaging and strategy. This will take time and resources to be successful, and will take away from your focus on what's already working.

If you have people coming on to your list who maybe can't quite afford the core offer you're selling, don't let it stress you out. Continue to nurture them and they will either eventually be able to afford your offer, or you can create something for them in the future. If you continue to nurture your audience, then when the time comes to launch something new, you have an existing audience to sell to.

When it's time to create a new product or funnel, because your other one is converting and making a million dollars as well as running on its own, adding to your value ladder is a great option. The mistake people make is they think they need a completed value ladder, with several offers ready for the audience within the first few months of starting to market their business. Creating a future offer that serves the same audience you're already having success with is an effective strategy because it keeps you focused on your proven audience. Just don't try to do it too soon.

You may never have a value ladder that's filled out, and that's okay. There are many successful businesses I know of, including my own, that don't have a completed value ladder and are making multiple seven figures a year.

Don't make the mistake of forcing yourself to create content and offers just to fill your value ladder. This will most likely result in poor quality offers being created as well as your attention and budget being spread across multiple offers confusing your audience and making it so everything converts okay but nothing converts amazing. You might think having a completed value ladder is the answer to you getting your business to the next level but it could actually do the opposite.

Never Lose Sight of the Long Game

True business success happens when the long game is constantly the focus. There is no such thing as overnight successes or "get rich quick" strategies that work and are sustainable. Everything you do today to build your audience, grow your email list, and increase the awareness of your brand, is building up to something even bigger. If you're able to see this and stick it out for the long run, you will experience the snowball effect where things start to take off quickly. This happens when you've been growing your audience consistently through content, and all of a sudden you have followers who have been connected to you for months and decide to purchase your offer. This happens when you have people sitting on your email list who signed up for your webinar six months ago, and now it's the right time for them to buy your offer, so they do. These people become paying customers, and you may have paid to attract them to your brand months ago when they weren't ready to buy. Now, all of a sudden, they are, and you get the sale that adds to your overall profit without you spending anything additional that month.

You will be able to tap into this snowball effect if you're consistent with your audience. This means you consider the long game in your strategy and brand growth. How are you going to continue to stay top of mind for your audience? How are you going to have additional touchpoints with your webinar registrants or challenge participants after the webinar or challenge is over? How are you going to build trust, not month over month, but year over year with your audience?

I have people who have followed my brand for three years and just signed up as a client or purchased my program because it was finally the right time for them. We have a client, we'll call her Ashley, who, after eight years of launching her signature program, reviewed her data and discovered the majority of people purchase her program after being on her list for a whole year. If you give up after a month, or you only look at the immediate money you make while building your business, you're missing the bigger picture of what you're building and ultimately missing out on a lot of potential customers and revenue.

A real and sustainable business is one where people have been following the brand for years and sales are coming in from all over the place because of that snowball effect. Your goal is to get your funnel so it's converting to sales and profits from the leads coming in in the short term. The snowball effect will then be the icing on the cake when you begin getting extra sales from followers and leads that have been sitting there this whole time. If you're willing to not lose patience and consistently look at the bigger picture of your business and marketing strategy, you will experience massive pay off.

Don't Make These Common Mistakes

The key to creating marketing success in your business is following everything I've taught you in *The Hirsh Process* and forcing yourself to be honest about these common mistakes, so you avoid making them.

After countless conversations and experiences with our clients and entrepreneurs just like you I can confidently tell you that these common mistakes are a major reason a business either doesn't grow or stops growing. As entrepreneurs, we often have to get out of our own way and all of these common mistakes are your opportunity to focus on what will work, get out of your own way and grow your company so that it reaches its highest potential.

Sometimes you will have to think twice and question yourself *when* that new funnel sounds like a brilliant idea or you start to fill your schedule up with too much day-to-day work and start losing your traction with your content and connection with your audience. *Hold yourself accountable* and avoid these mistakes so you don't slow down your long-term growth.

Amazing impact and an abundance of sales are in the palm of your hand if you follow all of the strategies I've laid out for you. Remember, stick to *The Hirsh Process*!

Chapter 10: How To Make It Easier

If you've made it this far and begun to navigate how you will create a marketing strategy that makes you both money and impact, then you've probably come to realize that creating a successful strategy is no easy feat. There are many components to a marketing strategy, and it's easy to get into a state of overwhelm about all of the moving parts. It's almost impossible to nail your strategy on the first try and sometimes it's going to feel extremely hard and overwhelming to navigate all of the different pieces.

I started my company when it was just me supporting clients with their Facebook ads. I was doing the strategy, the daily optimizing, the ad copy, all of it. This was not a sustainable business model and I knew that to grow, I would have to grow a team to serve my clients. During the process of growing a team and adding various skill sets onto my team, I came to realize there are three different skill sets a successful marketing campaign needs to be successful:

1. A high-level foundational strategy to make sure the funnel and messaging is going to convert when traffic is sent to it
2. Day-to-day optimization of the ads so that data is constantly being reviewed and decisions are being made around what to optimize, what

> to turn off, and what to change about the ads based on numbers

3. Creating ad copy and creative that will attract and convert the brand's ideal audience

As I continued to grow my team and serve my clients, I realized that a single person usually doesn't have all three of these skill sets, including myself. It's hard to find somebody who excels at both analytical thinking as well as highly creative thinking because these functions are in different parts of the brain.

My solution to this was to continually add on support to our client's accounts with multiple different experts. Today, each one of our clients has a mini team on their account, supporting them with their strategy and paid ads, so we can fully cover these three crucial pieces.

I followed my advice for over two years and my only offer in my business was to work with people as a direct client with our agency. My team supports them and handles all of their marketing so all they have to do is create content and be the visionary in their business. I obsessed over our delivery and systems and getting my team to a place where it runs itself, with me completely removed from the day-to-day. It took me two years to go from me doing everything, to fully out of the day-to-day and having very little involvement with the clients we serve. By the time I was able to achieve this, my company had hit a $3M run rate. Do you see why I am so passionate about focusing on one offer and one strategy? I followed this rule myself, even though there were a few times I almost broke it, and it was one of the best things I could have done for my company's growth.

Once I reached the place where my team was running itself and serving our clients, I knew I could focus on doing something that had been on my mind for the last year, which was building an online training program. All this time, I knew I was growing a following of people who weren't ready to be a client of our agency, but that I could greatly support with their marketing using all of our strategies, processes, and tools we use with clients. The three main marketing components that our agency clients need are also the ones I realized my students need. It doesn't matter what level of business you're at, there are strategies and core foundations that will always be relevant. Coming back to these three components and making sure you have them all nailed down will always be effective.

I had seen a lot of marketing and Facebook ad courses being sold in the market, but I had yet to see one that fully combined these three elements and didn't leave one or more out. You can't have a successful Facebook ad strategy without the big-picture marketing and sales funnel strategy, and you can't have a successful Facebook ad or funnel strategy without the messaging and creative nailed down. It took my team and me nearly a year of strategizing and building, but we created an online course that shows people how to create successful and customized marketing strategies, how to run traffic to those strategies, and how to optimize and scale them day in and day out.

I wanted to make sure our students saw success with their marketing, so instead of just giving away digital training and tools, I created live support in the program so that students could come and ask specific questions about their marketing and business. Some of the most powerful pieces of our online training program are not the content and information itself, but the live calls where students come and share their ads manager and stats and we help them with the next steps they need to take.

We've had hundreds of people go through our online course, and I won't say teaching is something I enjoy more than serving clients, because I love doing both, but I love teaching. I love supporting people with their marketing and helping them achieve the success I know they're capable of, but they are oftentimes intimidated by the overwhelm of digital marketing. I recently had a student on one of our coaching calls casually tell me she was going to build out a course, because she was getting so many leads on her list and into her funnel for her high-level service who weren't ready for that offer. I questioned her decision on this, even though she wasn't asking me if it was a good idea and was instead telling me that's what she was going to do.

I asked her if the funnel for her higher-level service was making money and was profitable. She said yes. I asked her if the funnel for her higher-level service funnel had fully tapped it's potential and was scaling without her involved. She said no. I asked her if she had opti-mized the funnel to get the most leads she could into her funnel selling her higher-level service. She said no, she was spending still only a small amount on ads. I asked her if she even had the bandwidth to create a new course, let alone market it. She said no.

She didn't decide on the call about what she was going to do, and I didn't push her into making a decision, but I could tell she was thinking about all I had said. Within a few hours after the call, she posted in our course Facebook group that for the rest of the year all she was going to do was focus on her higher-level service, and not only perfecting that funnel but also on streamlining the delivery of that service. Her post to the group told us that this was a life-changing moment in her business that she would not have had if she and I didn't have that conversation on the call.

To be a part of somebody's experience and growth in that way is one of the greatest rewards for me. I don't tell you this to brag about my ability to coach our students with our process, I tell you because you could so easily find yourself in her place. This student could have potentially wasted thousands of dollars and hours, trying to add in a new offer and a new funnel that was going to distract her and take away from what was already working and stall her overall growth.

The really interesting part was that she was already a part of our program, had watched all the training videos, and she was even one of my die-hard followers who listens to my podcast and knows my stance on the importance of focus in your business. None of those things mattered or registered with her. It took her having a conversation with me and talking through her idea to change her business and refocus herself for the rest of the year. I know for a fact this decision she made will make her more money and bring her more business success than if she would have gone the other direction. What if she hadn't reached out for help at that moment on that training call? Making mistakes is part of the process, and we all learn from our mistakes, but think how much time and money that saved my student, not making that one decision.

I love watching people personally grow and expand themselves and their businesses by working on and optimizing their marketing strategy. Your marketing strategy is connected to everything else in your business. Oftentimes, success is found on the other side of a massive breakthrough as my student had. Sometimes it doesn't always directly correlate to marketing but instead is about getting support with one of the hardest things we are all doing, growing a successful business.

If you feel overwhelmed or like you don't have enough support with your marketing and business and would like more support, I have a free community I've created for people who read this book. I will be inside that community as well, as will so many amazing entrepreneurs like you. You can sign up to join us here: hirshmarketinginsiders.com

And if you feel like you need more support with your marketing and would like access to our extensive video trainings, templates, swipe files and live coaching inside of Ignite you can learn more about that program here: www.ignitecourse.com

Chapter 11: Create Your Impact

Iknow you have a dream to not just make millions of dollars but to have an impact in this world that is greater than just you. I know what drives you is not just a healthy bank account but is the freedom that comes from making money and the lives you change as a result of that impact.

The hardest part of growing a business is often showing up every day, even when things feel hard. If anyone ever tells you that growing a successful business is easy, they haven't done it. Growing a successful business requires you to become a better version of yourself every day. To push yourself outside of your comfort zone and make decisions that are often difficult to make. If you've read this far, you were made for this, and I have no doubt you will go on to create an abundance of both profit and impact in your business.

I've always been so fascinated by marketing and growing an audience, especially once I saw the possibility with my client and his membership site that exploded in front of our eyes. From that moment on, I realized that if somebody has life-changing content to share with the world, they are doing a disservice to their audience by *not* marketing it to people daily.

Marketing is the key to building the business of your dreams, as well as an audience of people who value what you offer and the unique expertise you bring to the world. Used strategically, marketing will allow you to build an audience of followers who don't just represent a number on your Facebook page, but represent a genuine connection you've made using your content. The audience you strategically build will represent people who need what you have to offer, and from here on out, you *must* serve them.

When you started reading this book, you probably came in knowing your ultimate goal was to have a successful business that makes you millions of dollars someday. You also most likely knew that to do that, you had to figure out how to use digital marketing and Facebook ads strategically and effectively. What you may not have realized is how much of this success was already at your fingertips. Wherever you are now in your business, you can start creating a successful marketing strategy today, using everything I've taught you. There is nothing else standing between you and that success, besides yourself and the commitment you're willing to make to achieve it.

If you need to start with or revisit the foundational work that must happen before you run ads, then start by defining your ideal customer and defining the problem you solve for them. Then, define what marketing success looks like in your business, using both a custom marketing strategy and specific goals you can use to measure your success. If you've done the pre-work and you're clear on who it is you're trying to reach, you can start creating content to connect with your audience. You can make a commitment right now to release regular podcasts or videos, so your followers become an audience of true believers and selling becomes easy and effortless. Putting your brand out there consistently is not an easy commitment to make, but it will immediately help you connect with and build your audience.

If not now, then soon, you can start to hone in on a lead generation strategy that grows your email list. Not just to grow the number on your email list as a metric to show your friends, but because when you follow the process, those leads will become sales, and are a core piece to creating a much bigger impact. Once you're bringing quality leads into your business, sales are easy. Why? Because now that you're looking at everything in your marketing as a journey and an opportunity to connect with your audience, you can look at your sales this way too. Your next step might be to create strategic follow-ups and touchpoints with your brand so that all of those leads have no question that their next step is to purchase what you have to offer.

Finally, once you're growing your audience and getting consistent leads into your funnel, you can start to experience the real magic where marketing results become numbers, and you won't stop until you create that ATM that consistently spits out more than you spend on ads. All of the success and impact you've ever dreamed of is right at your fingertips. Many people lose focus or give up after a few weeks of what feels like failure. You're not going to be one of those people. You're not going to be one of those people because I've proven to you that "failing" in your marketing, just becomes data and a lesson that you learn for next time.

Failing and feeling frustrated or stuck is part of the process and path to success. The first time you feel like you're failing with your marketing, or like it's not working for you, I want you to take a deep breath, stop, and say to yourself, "This is supposed to be happening, I am on the right track."

If you can push through these feelings of fear and failure, you will unlock the next level in your business. Your job from here on out is to continually do the work on yourself to become the person your business needs you to be tomorrow. You now have the power and tools in front of you to go and create your impact. That's what I want for all of you, it's time for you to stop playing small, to stop treating your marketing and business growth as a side project, and to truly step up and create the impact you were born to create.

Are you ready?

Companion Exercises

Chapter 4: Identifying Your Ideal Customer

(Reference Page: 18)

Fill out the following relevant information about the ideal customer you're trying to attract:

Age:

Gender:

General Description (think about giving them a name and describing them as if they are a friend of yours):

Their Core Problem (described in 1 very clear sentence):

Their Dream Come True (described in 1 very clear sentence):

A list of problems they might complain about to their friends or family:

Their fears and worries that might keep them up at night:

Their biggest objections to purchasing what you sell:

Books they would read:

Podcasts they would listen to:

Chapter 4: Setting Your Ad Budget

(Reference Page: 18)

Exercise 1: Digital Products & Services

Follow these steps if you have a lead generation funnel such as a webinar, challenge or video series:

1. How much money do you want to make selling your product or service in one month?
2. Divide that amount of money by the cost of your product or service
3. How much (in units) of your product or service do you need to sell? (Example; 10 digital courses or 5 new clients)
4. What percentage of your email leads do you believe will purchase your offer? (Reference the table on page 29)
5. Once you have that percentage, how many email leads do you need to add to your list to sell the number you came up with in step 3?
6. What do you believe you'll be paying as an average cost per email lead? (Reference the table on page 29)
7. Multiply that average cost per lead by the number of email leads you need to meet your sales goal (answer to step 5). This is your ad budget to achieve your sales goal:

At the end of this exercise, you should have the following numbers defined for your first month of running ads:

- How much money will you make?

- How many sales will you sell in units?

- How many leads do you need to add to your email list?

- How much will you spend to accomplish all of this?

Exercise 2: Applications For High Ticket Sales:

Follow these steps if you're trying to get applications to book a call with you or your sales team so you can pitch your offer:

1. How much money do you want to make selling your product or service in one month?
2. Divide that amount of money by the cost of your product or service
3. How many sales do you need to make of this product or service? Ex; 5 new clients or 15 sales)
4. What percentage of your applications do you believe will purchase your offer? (Reference the table on page 29)
5. Once you have that percentage, how many applications do you need to sell the number you came up with in step 3?
6. What do you believe you'll be paying as an average cost per application?

7. Multiply that average cost by the number of applications you need to meet your sales goal (answer to step 5). This is your ad budget to achieve your sales goal:

At the end of this exercise, you should have the following numbers defined for your first month of ads:

- How much money will you make?
- How many people do you need to sell to achieve your goal?
- How many applications do you need?
- What is the cost per application you're aiming for?
- How much will you spend to accomplish all of this?

Exercise 3: E-commerce & Physical Products

Follow these steps if you are trying to sell a physical product:

1. How much money do you want to make selling your product in one month?
2. Divide that amount of money by the cost of your product or your average sale price (also known as average cart value) if you have multiple products:
3. How many sales do you need to make of this product?
4. Knowing your cost to ship and sell your product (your cost of goods), what is the maximum you

can pay to sell a product and still be profitable?

5. Multiply that maximum number by the amount of sales you want to make of your product, your answer to step 3, to get your total ad spend required to achieve your goal:

At the end of this exercise, you should have the following numbers defined for your first month of ads:

- How much money will you make?

- How many sales will you sell in units?

- What is the maximum you're willing to pay for a sale and still be profitable?

- How much will you spend to accomplish all of this?

** If these steps are unclear to you or you want to play around with different numbers, you can download our Facebook Ad Calculator here: www.fbadcalculator.com**

Chapter 5: Brand Awareness & Visibility: Choosing Your Content Creation Statement

(Reference Page: 32)

Follow these steps to create your content creation statement:

1. What type of content are you going to commit to creating that plays to your skill sets? Video, podcast, writing, etc.

2. How frequently are you going to release this content and on what platforms?

3. How much money are you going to spend promoting this content so new people see it? (Note: It should be 5-10% of your total marketing budget)

4. What is your final commitment statement? Some examples are:

   "I will release two podcast episodes a week and spend $25 each week promoting them so new people see them."

   "I will do a Facebook live video every Tuesday and Thursday and spend $50 each week promoting them to new audiences."

Chapter 6: Choosing Your Audiences To Target

(Reference Page: 42)

Follow these steps to make a list of 10-20 audiences you can target with your Facebook ads:

1. Think about 5 Facebook pages your ideal customer might like. These pages could be magazines they read, influencers they like, books they read, etc.

2. Navigate to audience insights in your ads managers and plug in your top audience that you chose from the list above into audience insights

3. Write down other pages that your audience may like based on the options that come up in audience insights

4. Repeat the above steps until you've created a final list of 10-20 audiences your ideal customer may follow on Facebook

5. Use these audiences to target your Facebook ads with and decide which ones convert the best based on the results you get back!

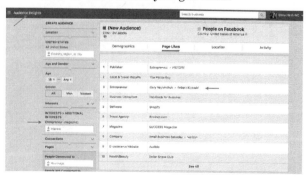

Chapter 7: Planning Your Retargeting Ads

(Reference Page: 59)

Follow these steps to plan out your retargeting ad strategy:

1. On a paper or whiteboard, draw out your completed customer journey with each step a lead would take to go from somebody who doesn't know you or your brand to a paying customer. This would include the content they may consume, the offers they may sign up for with their name & email and the product or service you offer.

2. At each action point in your customer journey where you want somebody to take an action, mark it as a place where you can place a retargeted ad

3. Create a final list of retargeted ads you will create with the audiences you'll target each retargeted ad with

4. Write and create ads that speak to each specific group of people based on previous actions they took (Example, a specific ad for somebody who signed up for your webinar but didn't watch it)

** Reference page 63 for examples of various retargeting ads to give you ideas **

Acknowledgements

Since I was ten years old, I've dreamed of becoming an author. I would write a book, staple it together, and hand it out to my family and friends, pretending I was a real author. I knew one day this dream would come true, and I'm so honored to put the last four years of experience of running marketing campaigns for clients into a book that I know will help many people succeed in their own business.

To my husband, who has supported me with every dream and every goal I've ever had. Thank you for breaking the rules with me and for being my partner in crime as we conquer the world together. Thank you for allowing me to turn my book-writing adventure into a mini-vacation and agreeing to be super-dad for a week while I wrote my book in Hawaii, even if you rolled your eyes when I told you I was going to Hawaii to write a book. Your dedication to our kids and family fills me with love and appreciation every day.

To Oliver, who was the biggest surprise, but yet greatest gift I've ever been handed by the universe. Thank you for making me a mom and being the catalyst for me to build this business and create the life of our dreams. Your sensitivity, love, and intelligence are incredible to witness and I'm so grateful to be your mom. To Ella, watching you own your independence since the day you came out has been humbling. You're my soul multiplied by ten, and allowing you to be you is one of my biggest priorities in life. Both of you are my inspiration, my motivation, and my heart. Thank you for showing me a love I didn't even know existed before you came into existence.

To this baby who was growing inside of me while I wrote this book. I know your entrance into this world will be a life-changing experience, and I can't wait to meet you and learn from you.

To my funnel bestie, Lindsay Padilla, who went on this book-writing journey with me and powered through our two-and-a-half-days-straight writing retreat in Hawaii. We made it to the other side together, and I don't know if I could have done it without you. My entrepreneur journey wouldn't be the same without you, our inside jokes, and all of our trips combining both fun and business.

To my mom, who has put her kids first since the moment she became a mom. Your dedication to your family is something I strive for every day. Thanks for showing me that you create your reality and can have anything you want when you take control of your life. The strength and willpower you've given me is a gift that I'll never be able to put into words. I know my strong-willed personality was not always easy to parent, but it's paid off as an adult. I can only hope to be the mom you were to us for my kids.

To my dad, who gave me the "entrepreneur gene" and is a constant outlet for me to talk about business and life with when I need. Thanks for always entertaining my nontraditional ideas about school and life growing up, and for supporting me when I wanted to break the rules.

To my three younger brothers, Brady, Matthew, and Brennan, who made me into the leader I am today and never fail to make me laugh. I love you guys and our endless memories and inside jokes.

To my entire team at Hirsh Marketing, who serve our clients and create an impact bigger than I ever could myself. Thank you for constantly pushing me to be a better leader and being willing to grow alongside me.

To Alex Charfen, who forced me to write *The Hirsh Process* and grow my team beyond whatever I ever thought I was capable of. Your mentorship and friendship have had a huge impact on both my personal and professional growth. I'm forever thankful that you allow me to push back on everything you say until I finally realize you are right and listen.

Finally, to every woman out there who has chosen to go against what society tells you you're "supposed to do" and instead committed themselves to creating their reality. To the moms who are willing to go after their dreams and have it all, without having to do it all.

About the Author

Emily Hirsh is a leading Digital Marketing Strategist and the CEO of Hirsh Marketing, one of the largest and fastest-growing digital marketing companies in the world. Emily and her team of experts work with top-level influencers and game-changing entrepreneurs to grow their businesses and generate massive revenue using her revolutionary system, *The Hirsh Process.*

In 2012, Emily and her husband, a master kettle-bell trainer, started an online fitness business together. By default, he was the content creator, and Emily was everything else. She managed social media, customer service, landing pages, graphics, outreach, sales funnels, and marketing.

She soon discovered digital marketing was her power zone, and the business quickly grew its following astronomically. Through pure grit, Emily unintentionally became an expert on all things business management, systems, and online marketing strategy. She slowly started taking on more clients, helping them grow their businesses, beyond their wildest dreams.

Since then, Emily has built a team of 30+ top-level strategists, ads managers, copywriters, graphic designers, and marketers to generate hundreds of thousands in ROI for her clients, every single month. They've managed over $18 million in ad spend and generated over $100 million in revenue for their clients. As an entrepreneur herself, Emily knows exactly what other business owners need to grow, reduce overwhelm and thrive happily in their zones of genius.

Emily is also the host of *The Hirsh Marketing Underground* podcast and can be found regularly traveling the country with her husband and two kids. In her spare time, she enjoys kettlebell training, being in nature, and reading novels.

Website: https://www.hirshmarketing.com/
Email: team@emilyhirsh.com
Facebook: https://www.facebook.com/hirshmarketing/
Instagram: http://instagram.com/emilyhirsh
Podcast: https://www.hirshmarketing.com/podcast/

Thank You

I love each of you who opened this book and committed to reading it from the introduction to the conclusion. You rock!

As a thank you, I've created a free training based on *The Hirsh Process* that you can take today and use to create and strategize your marketing strategy. Sign up at: hmfreetraining.com.

I'm so passionate about helping entrepreneurs fulfill their true potential and achieve the impact they were born to make. Hope you find this bonus training helpful!

I would love to hear any of your stories or even struggles as you implement *The Hirsh Process* in your own business and marketing. You can email team@emilyhirsh.com to share these stories and a chance to be featured in a later edition of this book.

Made in the USA
Columbia, SC
08 February 2021

32554208R00079